The Mind-Body Nexus:
Integrating Psychology and Physiology in Healing Trauma

Kenny Ajayi

Table of Contents

Chapter 1
Introduction

In the depths of our being, where memories linger like shadows and emotions echo through our veins, lies a realm often misunderstood yet profoundly powerful: the domain of trauma. It's a journey through the labyrinth of the mind, where the echoes of past pains reverberate through our very being, shaping our perceptions, our interactions, and our very existence.

The effects of trauma are like a ghost that haunts the lives of many people. Even though it's not something we can see or touch, this force has an effect on us that goes deep into our minds and bodies. When an intense event or series of events breaks our sense of safety, security, and control, we have what is called trauma. The quick death of a loved one, the horrors of war, or the sneaky hold of abuse are all things that can cause trauma that can't be erased.

"The Mind Body Nexus" is a powerful call to look into the deep links between the brain, mind, and body when it comes to getting better after tragedy. It invites us to look deeper than the surface of our bodies and into the maze-like depths of our humanity, where mental scars are deep and strength grows in the face of hardship.

Trauma comes in many forms and upsets the balance between the mind and body, leaving it in a state of pain, fear, and separation. However, as the book will show you, the body is not just a silent observer after stress; it is an important part of the process of healing and repair. Neurobiology, psychology, and physiology all work together to make sense of and process the stressful events that shape our lives.

On the other hand, survivors have shown how strong the human spirit is by showing that change and growth are possible even in the face of great hardship.

Oftentimes, those who have survived trauma must navigate the self-wilderness on their own, with feelings of sadness and hopelessness acting as guiding lights. The disjointed parts of the soul desire to be whole again on this journey. For those who have walked the harrowing paths of trauma, the journey to healing is often a solitary pilgrimage, a voyage through the wilderness of the self where the compass points are obscured by the fog of anguish and despair. It's a journey marked by shattered fragments of self, where the pieces of a shattered soul yearn to find cohesion once more.

Even though it's dark, there is a spark of hope—a light that shows the way to healing and repair. The book is meant to be a lighthouse, a road plan through the knotted maze of trauma, giving comfort to people who have felt like the weight of the world is on their shoulders.

As we set out on this trip to find out more about ourselves, let us remember that healing is a process, not a goal. It is a journey that starts with each breath, every heartbeat, and every moment of tender self-compassion. So, dear reader, in this profound exploration of the human condition, may you find solace in the knowledge that you are not alone—that amidst the chaos and the clamor, there exists a sanctuary, an embrace of our shared humanity. It is amazing how we find the courage to confront our demons and to emerge, transformed, into the light.

Trauma & Stress – The Dance of Domains

Trauma, psychology, and the intricate workings of the mind form a complex dominion that intertwines experience, emotion, and the physical body. It's a journey through the depths of our being where every domain has its distinct existence and, thus, its own distinct impact on the body.

Stress emerges as a central player in this ballet of domains, leaving lasting imprints on our mind and body, shaping our perceptions, actions, and self-perceptions. It's not merely a memory; stress becomes an entrenched emotion, reshaping our very outlook on the world and ourselves.

In psychology, trauma is often viewed as a disruption of our mental equilibrium, a breach in the defenses of our psyche that exposes us to overwhelming emotions and experiences. It leaves behind wounds that linger in the recesses of our minds, altering our worldview and sense of self.

Yet, the impact of stress transcends the confines of the mind, leaving a profound imprint on every facet of our physical being. Trauma manifests itself in a myriad of ways, from heightened vigilance to tangible signs of stress etched onto our bodies. Our physical selves silently bear the scars of our pain long after the initial wounds have healed.

The intricate dance between mind and body is where the echoes of pain reverberate, forging a symbiotic relationship between thought and sensation. Our thoughts shape our perceptions, which in turn influence our bodily responses, perpetuating a cycle of stress and its repercussions.

Ultimately, the recognition of our interconnectedness—with each other, with our traumas, and with the world around us—empowers us to confront our vulnerabilities and embrace our imperfections. True strength emerges in the sacred space where psychology intersects with physiology, where the mind converges with the body, and where pain becomes a catalyst for change. Only after understanding what's hurting us, we can begin the process of healing.

Intersectionality of Trauma

The complexity of trauma reveals the intricate and deeply intertwined nature of the human experience. Within lies the thirst for identity, power, and privilege, combining together to shape both pain and resilience. At the intersection where oppression and marginalization converge, trauma emerges as a complex system differing on the basis of race, ethnicity, gender, sexuality, class, and more, illustrating how power dynamics and systemic injustices shape our sociology.

For marginalized communities, trauma is often exacerbated by systemic inequities and historical injustices. The wounds of abuse leave scars on the collective psyche, echoing through generations. Persistent racism, sexism, homophobia, transphobia, and the enduring legacies of colonialism and slavery compound the suffering experienced by minority groups, amplifying the impact of multiple layers of oppression. For instance, individuals from underrepresented groups may encounter barriers to accessing mental health care and support services due to cultural stigma, language barriers, and distrust of conventional institutions. Traumatic events are also shaped by community norms, values, and coping mechanisms, influencing help-seeking behaviors and perceptions of mental health and illness.

The intersectionality of trauma underscores the intricate interplay between various forms of injustice and power dynamics within individuals' lives and communities. Individuals with marginalized identities may face intersecting traumas, such as racial trauma compounded by sexism or homophobia, while those with privileged identities may perpetuate harm through abuse or neglect, exacerbating the pain experienced by disadvantaged groups.

An intersectional understanding of trauma calls upon us to embrace a broader perspective of human suffering and resilience—one that embraces the complexity of lived experiences, acknowledges the intertwined nature of privilege and oppression, and affirms the inherent worth and dignity of every individual and community. To forge a path toward healing, justice, and liberation for all, we must adopt an intersectional lens that illuminates the interconnectedness of our shared humanity.

Stigma Surrounding Mental Health

Imagine a world where pain and suffering hide in the shadows, where speaking up about mental health feels like a forbidden act. It's a reality where stigma lurks, casting shame and silence upon those who struggle with mental illness.

Stigma, at its core, thrives on ignorance and fear. It's the voice that labels and ostracizes those whose experiences differ from the norm. It drills its way through our society, shaping beliefs and actions and pushing those who suffer into the margins of our communities.

For too long, mental illness has been shrouded in secrecy, discussed only in hushed tones. Its victims find themselves isolated, unable to seek the support they desperately need. This culture of silence not only perpetuates the stigma but also denies individuals access to care, employment, and social inclusion, trapping them in cycles of despair and loneliness.

Yet after all the prejudice, after all the so-called minimal effort to understand mental health, people are rising up, demanding change and understanding. They are challenging the status quo, advocating for mental health awareness, and breaking down the barriers of stigma.

Education has become the beacon of light in this fight against shame. By sharing knowledge stories of resilience and fostering open dialogue, we chip away at the walls that stigma has built. But education alone is not enough. We must also push for systemic changes, ensuring equal access to mental health care and dismantling the structures that perpetuate discrimination.

At its essence, this book is a battle against enforced shame, a battle for our humanity—for compassion, understanding, and fairness in the face of adversity. We must stand with those who struggle, amplifying their voices and rejecting the narratives of silence and shame. Together, through unity, kindness, and determination, we can confront the effects of trauma and forge a future where everyone is seen, heard, and treated with dignity and justice.

What is the Purpose of this Book

This book serves as a beacon of clarity in the often-bewildering realm of trauma and its repercussions. It endeavors to unlock the mysteries of trauma by painting a comprehensive portrait of its impact on people's lives.

At its core, the book aims to illuminate the intricate interplay between the brain, mind, and body during times of stress and recovery. Trauma, a multifaceted subject, exerts profound effects on mental health, relationships, and overall well-being. Drawing from decades of professional expertise, scientific inquiry, and personal narratives, this book offers readers invaluable insights into this complex phenomenon. It aims to accomplish several main goals:

Understanding Trauma

Imagine you're standing at the edge of a dark forest, surrounded by shadows that seem to whisper secrets of the past. This is where our journey begins—a journey into the depths of human experience, where trauma lurks like a hidden beast waiting to pounce.

In this book, we delve into the heart of trauma, exploring its many faces and the profound impact it leaves on our lives. From the sudden jolt of unexpected events to the silent erosion of long-term stress, trauma takes on many forms, each leaving its own indelible mark on our souls.

But what lies beneath the surface of trauma? What happens to our minds and bodies when faced with danger and hardship? It's a question that cuts to the core of our humanity, revealing the intricate dance between our brains and our emotions.

Through the lens of neuroscience, we uncover the hidden mechanisms of trauma, unraveling the tangled web of neural pathways that shape our thoughts and actions. We learn how our brains instinctively respond to threats, triggering a cascade of physiological reactions that can alter the very fabric of our being.

Exploring the Mind-Body Connection

Picture yourself standing in front of a mirror, looking not just at your reflection but into the depths of your being. In this book, we uncover a profound truth: the mind and body are not separate entities but intertwined threads of our existence, especially when facing stress and trauma.

Think about the last time you felt overwhelmed, your heart racing, your breath shallow. These physical sensations are not mere coincidences but manifestations of the turmoil within. Stress leaves its fingerprints on our bodies, weaving a complex tapestry of physical signs and somatic issues that speak volumes about our inner struggles.

From headaches to stomach pains, from tense muscles to restless nights, our bodies bear the scars of our emotional battles. But it's not just about the symptoms; it's about understanding the deeper connection between our mental discomfort and physical experience.

By peeling back the layers of our existence, this book reveals how trauma leaves its mark on every fiber of our being. It's a journey of self-discovery, a mirror held up to our souls, reflecting the ways in which trauma has shaped our lives.

Charting a Path to Healing

Imagine standing at the edge of a vast landscape, with the weight of the world pressing down on your shoulders. In the pages of this book, discover hope—a roadmap to healing that acknowledges the immense challenges posed by stress and trauma.

Explore a myriad of therapeutic approaches, each offering a glimmer of possibility in the darkness. From the tangible realm of physical experiences to the ethereal realms of mindfulness, uncover a tapestry of healing modalities waiting to be embraced.

Mind-body methods intertwine and give rise to a path to healing. Through the gentle practice of mindfulness and the profound connection between our thoughts and sensations, we discover the power to reclaim our stories and rewrite our destinies.

But healing is not a destination—it's a journey, a process of self-discovery and transformation. With each step forward, we reclaim a piece of ourselves, piecing together the fragments of our shattered selves, eventually becoming whole again.

In these pages, you'll find not just words but a guiding light—a reminder that you are not alone in your journey.

Advocating for Social Change

Imagine a world where compassion reigns supreme, where every corner is infused with the warmth of understanding and connection. This is the vision that pulses at the heart of "The Mind Body Nexus."

It beckons us to envision a society where communities and structures are built upon a foundation of empathy and sensitivity—a world where healing is not just a privilege but a fundamental human right. Through his impassioned plea, he ignites a spark of awareness, urging us to confront the pervasive impact of trauma in our midst. But this is more than a call to action; it's a uniting cry for kindness, understanding, and social justice.

Resilience and Coping

Imagine trauma and healing as a complicated dance, where resilience and coping are partners guiding us through the uncomfortable challenges of life. Together, they embody the essence of the human mind—the ability to endure, adapt, and emerge stronger in pursuit of health and happiness.

Resilience, at its core, is the innate capacity within each of us to bounce back after setbacks, to navigate life's storms with grace and fortitude, and to emerge from them even more resilient than before. It's the glimmer of hope in the darkest of nights, the beacon that guides us through moments of despair.

Coping, on the other hand, encompasses a wide array of methods and strategies we employ to navigate through adversity. From seeking social support to nurturing ourselves, from drawing on spiritual beliefs to finding meaning in suffering, coping strategies provide us with a sense of empowerment and control when life feels overwhelming.

Dealing with challenges and cultivating resilience are integral aspects of the healing journey. It demands courage, perseverance, and a steadfast determination to reclaim ownership of our narratives.

When faced with trauma, resilience guides us to the path of healing and transformation. It instills within us the belief that we possess the strength to overcome adversity.

Coping, meanwhile, serves as a lifeline during turbulent times, equipping us with the tools and knowledge to navigate the rough waters of stress with resilience and strength.

Moreover, resilience and coping foster personal growth and change, deepening our understanding of ourselves, cultivating empathy for others, and nurturing bonds within our communities. Through shared experiences of pain and hardship, we forge connections that foster a sense of belonging and solidarity.

As we conclude this introductory chapter, we stand at the threshold of an awakening—one of resilience, healing, and transformation.

In the pages that follow, we will delve deeper into the complexities of trauma, resilience, and coping, untying the knots that tie us to our past while guiding us toward a future filled with hope and possibility.

Chapter Two
The Nature of Trauma

Discerning Trauma

Trauma, at its core, constitutes far more than a mere distressing experience. It encapsulates the profound impact of events that exceed an individual's capacity to manage, thrusting them into a state of vulnerability and powerlessness. Broadly defined, trauma emerges from any occurrence or series of occurrences—ranging from sudden accidents to prolonged abuse—that shatters the equilibrium of one's psychological and emotional resilience. Such experiences imprint themselves upon the psyche, leaving indelible marks that persist long after the event has passed. It's crucial to understand that trauma extends beyond physical harm; it encompasses the complex interplay between the mind and emotions, deeply altering one's perceptions, behaviors, and sense of self.

The defining characteristic of trauma lies in its capacity to overwhelm the innate coping mechanisms of an individual, rendering them defenseless against the onslaught of distressing stimuli. This overwhelming nature distinguishes trauma from the typical challenges encountered in everyday life, as it penetrates the very core of one's being, disrupting the fundamental sense of safety and security. Whether it manifests as a single cataclysmic event or a sustained pattern of adversity, trauma inflicts wounds that transcend the physical realm, infiltrating the inner sanctum of the mind and soul.

Moreover, the aftermath of trauma reverberates through the fabric of an individual's existence, casting a shadow that extends far beyond the confines of the traumatic event itself. The emotional and psychological scars left in its wake serve as constant reminders of the harrowing ordeal endured. They manifest in myriad ways, from debilitating anxiety and pervasive fear to profound feelings of shame, guilt, and worthlessness. These residual effects permeate every facet of life, hindering relationships, impeding personal growth, and constraining one's capacity for joy and fulfillment.

Importantly, trauma is a deeply subjective experience shaped by the unique vulnerabilities, beliefs, and lived experiences of each individual. What may constitute trauma for one person might be perceived as a manageable challenge for another. Thus, the significance of trauma lies not solely in the event itself but in the profound impact it exerts on the individual's inner world. Acknowledging this inherent subjectivity underscores the importance of adopting a compassionate and nuanced approach to understanding and addressing trauma, recognizing that each person's journey toward healing is inherently unique.

In essence, trauma represents an existential rupture, a breach in the fabric of human existence that leaves in its wake a profound sense of disconnection and disarray. By acknowledging the complexities inherent in trauma's definition, we can begin to appreciate the depth of its impact and the urgency of cultivating spaces of healing and support for those who bear its burden. Only through empathy, understanding, and firm support can we hope to navigate the labyrinthine terrain of trauma and guide individuals toward a path of resilience, restoration, and renewal.

Types of Trauma

Trauma is a multifaceted phenomenon, encompassing a diverse array of experiences that profoundly impact individuals' lives. Understanding the distinct types of trauma is crucial for delineating the complexities of their effects on mental and emotional well-being. One such classification distinguishes between acute trauma and complex trauma, each characterized by unique features and implications for psychological health.

Acute trauma typically arises from sudden, often unforeseen events that pose an immediate threat to an individual's safety and well-being. Examples include accidents, natural disasters, and assaults. These incidents elicit intense fear, helplessness, or horror, overwhelming an individual's capacity to cope in the moment. The aftermath of acute trauma is often marked by a range of acute stress reactions, including flashbacks, nightmares, and hypervigilance. While these responses may gradually subside for some individuals with time and support, others may develop more enduring psychological symptoms indicative of post-traumatic stress disorder (PTSD).

In contrast, complex trauma involves prolonged or repetitive exposure to traumatic events, typically occurring within interpersonal relationships or environments characterized by chronic adversity. Common examples include childhood abuse or neglect, domestic violence, and ongoing community violence. Unlike acute trauma, complex trauma unfolds over an extended period, exerting a cumulative toll on an individual's psyche. The effects of complex trauma extend far beyond the immediate aftermath of the events, shaping the individual's identity, relationships, and worldview. Survivors of complex trauma often grapple with a myriad of challenges, including emotional dysregulation, dissociation, and difficulties in forming and maintaining healthy interpersonal connections.

What distinguishes complex trauma from its acute counterpart is the pervasive and enduring nature of its impact. While acute trauma may stem from isolated incidents, complex trauma is rooted in ongoing patterns of victimization, betrayal, and powerlessness. Consequently, the recovery journey for individuals affected by complex trauma is often protracted and arduous, requiring comprehensive therapeutic interventions that address the multifaceted layers of their experiences.

Moreover, the distinction between acute and complex trauma underscores the importance of adopting a holistic and nuanced approach to trauma-informed care. Recognizing the unique challenges faced by survivors of each type of trauma enables clinicians and caregivers to tailor interventions that align with the individual's specific needs and experiences. By fostering environments of safety, validation, and empowerment, we can support survivors on their path toward healing and resilience, transcending the shackles of trauma to reclaim agency, meaning, and vitality in their lives.

Common Reactions to Trauma

The aftermath of trauma often manifests in a myriad of emotional, cognitive, and behavioral responses, each reflecting the complex interplay between the individual's psyche and the traumatic event itself. These reactions serve as adaptive mechanisms aimed at coping with the overwhelming distress and threat posed by the traumatic experience. Among the most prevalent responses to trauma are flashbacks, wherein individuals vividly re-experience the traumatic event as if it were happening in the present moment. These intrusive memories can be triggered by various cues, such as sights, sounds, or even internal sensations, plunging individuals into a state of profound distress and disorientation.

Hypervigilance, another common reaction to trauma, entails a heightened state of alertness and arousal characterized by an increased sensitivity to potential threats in one's environment. Individuals afflicted by hypervigilance often find themselves constantly scanning their surroundings for signs of danger, unable to relax or let their guard down. This pervasive sense of vulnerability can significantly impair daily functioning, leading to difficulties in concentration, sleep disturbances, and a pervasive sense of exhaustion.

Furthermore, avoidance emerges as a prevalent coping strategy employed by individuals grappling with the aftermath of trauma. Whether consciously or unconsciously, survivors may seek to evade reminders of the traumatic event, be it through avoiding specific people, places, or activities associated with the trauma. While avoidance initially serves as a means of self-protection, it can ultimately impede the healing process, reinforcing feelings of isolation, shame, and emotional numbing.

Dissociation represents yet another common response to trauma, characterized by a detachment from one's thoughts, emotions, or surroundings. In moments of acute distress, individuals may dissociate as a means of escaping the overwhelming intensity of their emotions, effectively creating a psychological barrier between themselves and the traumatic event. However, while dissociation may offer temporary relief from distress, it can also fragment one's sense of self and exacerbate feelings of alienation and detachment from reality.

Collectively, these common reactions to trauma underscore the profound impact of such experiences on the individual's psyche and well-being. By elucidating the diverse array of responses that may ensue in the wake of trauma, we can cultivate greater empathy and understanding for those navigating the complexities of their trauma-related experiences. Moreover, by recognizing these reactions as adaptive responses to distress, we can provide survivors with the validation, support, and resources they need to embark on a journey of healing and recovery. Through fostering environments of safety, compassion, and empowerment, we can help survivors reclaim agency over their lives, transcending the shackles of trauma to forge a path toward resilience, growth, and renewal.

Individual Differences

The response to trauma is a deeply personal and nuanced experience, influenced by a myriad of individual factors that shape each person's unique journey toward healing and recovery. One of the key determinants of how individuals respond to trauma lies in their genetic makeup. Research has shown that genetic predispositions can play a significant role in modulating an individual's vulnerability to developing psychological disorders following traumatic experiences. Certain genetic variations may confer resilience, buffering individuals against the adverse effects of trauma, while others may increase susceptibility to conditions such as post-traumatic stress disorder (PTSD) or depression.

Personality traits also exert a profound influence on how individuals navigate the aftermath of trauma. For instance, individuals with high levels of resilience, characterized by traits such as optimism, adaptability, and self-efficacy, may exhibit greater psychological fortitude in the face of adversity. Conversely, those with predisposing factors such as neuroticism or negative emotionality may be more prone to experiencing heightened distress and maladaptive coping strategies following trauma. Moreover, personality traits can shape the individual's coping style, influencing whether they confront the trauma head-on or resort to avoidance and withdrawal as coping mechanisms.

Past experiences and life circumstances further contribute to the variability in individuals' responses to trauma. Childhood experiences, in particular, can profoundly shape one's capacity to cope with and recover from traumatic events later in life. Individuals who have experienced early adversity, such as abuse, neglect, or insecure attachment, may exhibit heightened vulnerability to trauma-related psychopathology. Additionally, cultural and socioeconomic factors can intersect with past experiences to influence coping strategies, help-seeking behaviors, and access to resources for recovery.

Moreover, the nature and severity of the traumatic event itself play a pivotal role in shaping individuals' responses. Factors such as the duration, intensity, and perceived threat of the trauma can influence the degree of psychological distress experienced. Furthermore, the presence of interpersonal support systems, such as family, friends, or community networks, can serve as a protective factor, mitigating the impact of trauma and facilitating resilience.

By acknowledging and understanding the myriad factors that contribute to individual differences in trauma response, clinicians and caregivers can adopt a more personalized and tailored approach to treatment and support. Recognizing the inherent variability in how people navigate the aftermath of trauma underscores the importance of fostering environments of empathy, validation, and cultural sensitivity. Through a holistic understanding of these individual differences, we can empower survivors to harness their innate strengths and resources in their journey toward healing and resilience.

The Impact of Trauma on the Brain and Body

Neurobiological Effects

Trauma exerts a profound influence on the intricate workings of the human brain, reshaping its structures and functions in ways that can have enduring implications for mental and emotional well-being. At the neural level, traumatic experiences can lead to alterations in key brain regions implicated in-memory processing, emotion regulation, and stress response. Among the most prominently affected structures are the amygdala, hippocampus, and prefrontal cortex, each playing a pivotal role in shaping the individual's response to stress and adversity.

The amygdala, often referred to as the brain's "fear center," serves as a crucial hub for processing and encoding emotionally salient information. In the context of trauma, the amygdala may become hyperactive, heightening the individual's sensitivity to potential threats and triggering exaggerated fear responses. This heightened reactivity can contribute to the development of symptoms such as hypervigilance, flashbacks, and emotional dysregulation, perpetuating a cycle of heightened arousal and distress.

Conversely, the hippocampus, a structure integral to memory formation and consolidation, can undergo structural changes in response to trauma. Chronic exposure to stress hormones, such as cortisol, may impair hippocampal function, leading to deficits in declarative memory and spatial navigation. As a result, individuals may experience difficulties in recalling specific details of the traumatic event or integrating fragmented memories into a cohesive narrative, contributing to the phenomenon of dissociation and fragmented recollections.

Furthermore, trauma can exert profound effects on the prefrontal cortex, a region critical for executive functions such as decision-making, impulse control, and emotion regulation. Dysregulation of prefrontal cortical circuits can compromise the individual's ability to modulate emotional responses and engage in adaptive coping strategies. This deficit in top-down regulation may contribute to symptoms of anxiety, depression, and impulsivity commonly observed in individuals with a history of trauma.

Moreover, the neurobiological effects of trauma extend beyond alterations in specific brain regions to encompass broader changes in neural connectivity and neurochemical signaling pathways. Dysregulation of the hypothalamic-pituitary-adrenal (HPA) axis, for example, can lead to prolonged elevation of stress hormone levels, perpetuating a state of chronic hyperarousal and dysregulation. Additionally, trauma-induced changes in neurotransmitter systems, such as serotonin and dopamine, may contribute to alterations in mood, reward processing, and behavioral responses to stress.

In summary, trauma's impact on the brain is multifaceted, encompassing alterations in brain structure, function, and neurochemical signaling. By elucidating the neurobiological underpinnings of trauma-related psychopathology, we can gain a deeper understanding of the mechanisms underlying individuals' responses to adversity. Moreover, this knowledge can inform the development of targeted interventions aimed at mitigating the neurobiological effects of trauma and promoting recovery and resilience in survivors.

Stress Response System

The stress response system is a complex network of physiological mechanisms designed to mobilize the body's resources in response to perceived threats or challenges. At the core of this system lies the hypothalamic-pituitary-adrenal (HPA) axis, a neuroendocrine pathway that orchestrates the body's hormonal response to stress. When confronted with a traumatic event, the hypothalamus, a region of the brain responsible for regulating various bodily functions, releases corticotropin-releasing hormone (CRH). This hormone acts on the pituitary gland, prompting it to release adrenocorticotropic hormone (ACTH) into the bloodstream.

Subsequently, ACTH travels to the adrenal glands, small organs located atop the kidneys, where it stimulates the production and release of stress hormones such as cortisol and adrenaline. Cortisol, often referred to as the body's primary stress hormone, plays a central role in mobilizing energy reserves, enhancing alertness, and modulating immune function. Elevated cortisol levels help prepare the body for action in the face of danger, facilitating responses such as increased heart rate, heightened vigilance, and heightened arousal.

In parallel to the HPA axis, the sympathetic nervous system (SNS) also plays a pivotal role in orchestrating the body's immediate response to stress. Activated by signals from the brainstem, the SNS triggers the release of adrenaline (epinephrine) and noradrenaline (norepinephrine) from the adrenal medulla. These neurotransmitters act as potent mediators of the body's fight-or-flight response, rapidly mobilizing resources to cope with imminent threats. Adrenaline increases heart rate, elevates blood pressure, and enhances muscle strength, preparing the individual to confront or evade danger.

While these physiological responses are adaptive in the short term, chronic or excessive activation of the stress response system can have detrimental effects on physical and mental health. Prolonged exposure to elevated cortisol levels, for example, has been linked to a range of adverse health outcomes, including immune suppression, metabolic disturbances, and cognitive impairments. Similarly, chronic activation of the sympathetic nervous system can contribute to cardiovascular problems, gastrointestinal disorders, and heightened anxiety or panic symptoms.

Moreover, the dysregulation of the stress response system is a hallmark feature of many stress-related psychiatric disorders, such as post-traumatic stress disorder (PTSD) and depression. Individuals with PTSD may exhibit alterations in HPA axis functioning, characterized by blunted cortisol responses to stress or exaggerated baseline cortisol levels. These disturbances in stress hormone regulation can contribute to symptoms such as hypervigilance, emotional dysregulation, and intrusive memories, perpetuating a cycle of heightened arousal and distress.

In summary, the hypothalamic-pituitary-adrenal axis and the sympathetic nervous system constitute integral components of the body's adaptive response to stress and trauma. By mobilizing energy reserves, enhancing alertness, and modulating physiological functions, these systems enable individuals to cope with acute threats and challenges. However, chronic or excessive activation of the stress response system can have detrimental effects on physical and mental health, highlighting the importance of promoting resilience and implementing strategies to mitigate the long-term impact of trauma on the body and mind.

Physical Health Consequences

The impact of trauma extends far beyond the realm of mental and emotional well-being, exerting profound effects on physical health and overall physiological functioning. Emerging research has increasingly recognized the intricate interplay between traumatic experiences and various physical health conditions, shedding light on the multifaceted pathways through which trauma can influence bodily systems. Among the most notable physical health consequences associated with trauma are cardiovascular disease, autoimmune disorders, and chronic pain, each representing distinct manifestations of the body's response to chronic stress and adversity.

Cardiovascular disease stands as one of the most well-documented physical health outcomes linked to trauma exposure. Chronic activation of the stress response system, characterized by elevated levels of stress hormones such as cortisol and adrenaline, can contribute to dysregulation of cardiovascular function, predisposing individuals to hypertension, atherosclerosis, and other cardiovascular risk factors. Moreover, the cumulative burden of psychological distress and emotional dysregulation associated with trauma may exacerbate lifestyle factors such as poor diet, sedentary behavior, and substance abuse, further amplifying the risk of cardiovascular morbidity and mortality.

Similarly, trauma has been implicated in the pathogenesis of autoimmune disorders, conditions characterized by aberrant immune responses directed against the body's own tissues. Dysregulation of the immune system, stemming from prolonged exposure to stress hormones and inflammatory mediators, can disrupt the delicate balance between immune tolerance and reactivity, increasing susceptibility to autoimmune conditions such as rheumatoid arthritis, lupus, and multiple sclerosis. Furthermore, adverse childhood experiences, including trauma and neglect, have been linked to alterations in immune function and inflammatory markers, underscoring the enduring impact of early-life stressors on immune health.

Chronic pain represents another common physical health consequence of trauma, often stemming from alterations in pain processing pathways and heightened sensitivity to nociceptive stimuli. Traumatic experiences can sensitize the nervous system, amplifying pain perception and lowering the pain threshold, leading to conditions such as fibromyalgia, chronic back pain, and migraines. Moreover, the psychological sequelae of trauma, including depression, anxiety, and post-traumatic stress disorder (PTSD), can exacerbate pain symptoms through mechanisms such as central sensitization, catastrophizing, and avoidance behaviors.

Furthermore, the link between trauma and physical health extends beyond individual pathology to encompass broader health disparities and inequities. Marginalized populations, including racial and ethnic minorities, socioeconomically disadvantaged individuals, and survivors of interpersonal violence, are disproportionately affected by trauma and its associated health consequences. Structural factors such as discrimination, poverty, and lack of access to healthcare further compound the burden of trauma-related morbidity and mortality, perpetuating cycles of inequality and injustice.

In summary, trauma exerts a profound influence on physical health, predisposing individuals to a range of conditions such as cardiovascular disease, autoimmune disorders, and chronic pain. By elucidating the complex pathways through which trauma impacts bodily systems, we can develop more comprehensive approaches to prevention, intervention, and treatment, addressing the interconnected nature of mental, emotional, and physical well-being. Moreover, by addressing social determinants of health and promoting resilience-building strategies, we can mitigate the adverse effects of trauma on vulnerable populations and foster environments of healing, empowerment, and equity.

Interpersonal Effects

The reverberations of trauma extend far beyond the individual, permeating the intricate bond of interpersonal relationships and social connections. Traumatic experiences can profoundly impact how individuals navigate and engage with others, giving rise to a myriad of challenges in trust, intimacy, and communication. At the heart of these interpersonal effects lies a fundamental disruption in the relational dynamics that underpin human connection, leaving individuals grappling with profound feelings of vulnerability, mistrust, and isolation.

One of the most notable consequences of trauma on interpersonal relationships is the erosion of trust. Traumatic experiences often shatter individuals' sense of safety and security, leaving them wary of opening up to others or relying on them for support. Trust, a cornerstone of healthy relationships, becomes fraught with uncertainty and apprehension as survivors grapple with pervasive doubts about others' intentions and reliability. This erosion of trust can hinder the development of close, meaningful connections, perpetuating a cycle of social isolation and emotional withdrawal.

Moreover, trauma can disrupt individuals' ability to form and maintain intimate relationships characterized by emotional closeness, vulnerability, and mutual support. Survivors may struggle with intimacy, fearing the vulnerability and emotional exposure that comes with forming deep connections with others. Past experiences of betrayal or interpersonal violence may further compound these difficulties, fostering a sense of relational guardedness and emotional distance. Consequently, individuals may find themselves trapped in cycles of avoidance or self-sabotage, unable to cultivate the intimate connections they desire.

Communication, too, bears the brunt of trauma's impact on interpersonal relationships. The ability to effectively communicate thoughts, feelings, and needs is crucial for fostering healthy, mutually satisfying connections with others. However, trauma can disrupt individuals' communication skills, leading to difficulties in expressing themselves openly and assertively. Survivors may struggle with verbalizing their emotions, navigating conflict, or setting boundaries in relationships, perpetuating misunderstandings and relational conflicts. Moreover, trauma-related symptoms such as hypervigilance, dissociation, or emotional numbness can further impede effective communication, hindering authentic connection and mutual understanding.

Furthermore, the interpersonal effects of trauma extend beyond individual relationships to encompass broader social functioning and community engagement. Trauma survivors may experience difficulties in socializing, participating in group activities, or seeking out support from peers and community resources. Stigmatization, shame, and fear of judgment may further isolate survivors, exacerbating feelings of loneliness and alienation. Consequently, individuals may withdraw from social interactions, limiting their opportunities for connection and support and perpetuating a sense of disconnection from the broader community.

In summary, trauma's impact on interpersonal relationships is profound and far-reaching, disrupting trust, intimacy, and communication in profound ways. By recognizing and addressing the interpersonal effects of trauma, we can create spaces of empathy, validation, and support for survivors, fostering healing and resilience in the context of relationships. Moreover, by promoting trauma-informed approaches to interpersonal dynamics and community engagement, we can cultivate environments that prioritize safety, trust, and connection, empowering survivors to rebuild and nurture meaningful connections with others.

The Evolution of Trauma Treatment:

Historical Perspective

The historical treatment of trauma reflects humanity's evolving understanding of psychological distress and its therapeutic management across different epochs and cultures. Early civilizations often attributed traumatic symptoms to supernatural forces or divine punishment, leading to various ritualistic practices aimed at exorcising evil spirits or appeasing deities. Among the most ancient forms of trauma treatment was trepanation, a surgical procedure involving the drilling or scraping of holes in the skull to release perceived demonic influences or restore balance to the afflicted individual's psyche.

In ancient Greece and Rome, trauma was conceptualized through the lens of humoral theory, which posited that imbalances in bodily fluids, or humors, were the root cause of mental and physical ailments. Treatment often revolved around restoring equilibrium through interventions such as bloodletting, purging, and herbal remedies. Additionally, philosophical schools such as Stoicism and Epicureanism offered insights into the nature of suffering and resilience, emphasizing the importance of cultivating inner strength and detachment from external events.

The advent of modern psychology in the late 19th and early 20th centuries ushered in a paradigm shift in the understanding and treatment of trauma. Sigmund Freud, the founder of psychoanalysis, revolutionized the field by introducing concepts such as repression, dissociation, and the unconscious mind. Freud's work laid the foundation for psychoanalytic approaches to trauma, which aimed to uncover and process unresolved conflicts and traumatic memories through techniques such as free association, dream analysis, and catharsis.

The aftermath of World War I and World War II witnessed a surge in interest and research into the psychological consequences of warfare and combat trauma. Psychiatrists such as William James, Pierre Janet, and John Bowlby made significant contributions to our understanding of trauma's impact on mental health and interpersonal relationships. Moreover, the development of early trauma therapies, including hypnosis, desensitization techniques, and psychodynamic interventions, paved the way for the emergence of modern trauma-focused treatments such as cognitive-behavioral therapy (CBT), eye movement desensitization and reprocessing (EMDR), and dialectical behavior therapy (DBT).

In contemporary times, trauma treatment has evolved to encompass a diverse array of evidence-based interventions that prioritize safety, empowerment, and collaboration. Trauma-informed care, grounded in principles of empathy, validation, and cultural sensitivity, seeks to create environments that foster healing and resilience for survivors of trauma. By integrating insights from neuroscience, psychology, and social sciences, trauma treatment continues to evolve, offering hope and support to those navigating the complex terrain of trauma and recovery.

Shift to Evidence-Based Approaches

The transition from anecdotal or speculative treatments to evidence-based interventions represents a pivotal shift in the field of mental health, signaling a movement toward empirically validated approaches grounded in scientific rigor and clinical efficacy. This paradigmatic evolution has been driven by a growing recognition of the limitations of traditional psychotherapeutic models and the need for standardized, replicable interventions that yield measurable outcomes. Among the most prominent evidence-based approaches to emerge in recent decades are cognitive-behavioral therapy (CBT), eye movement desensitization and reprocessing (EMDR), and dialectical behavior therapy (DBT), each offering distinct methodologies for addressing trauma and related psychological concerns.

Cognitive-behavioral therapy (CBT) represents a cornerstone of evidence-based practice, drawing upon principles of cognitive restructuring and behavioral modification to alleviate distressing symptoms and dysfunctional patterns of thinking and behavior. Rooted in the premise that maladaptive thoughts and beliefs contribute to emotional distress and behavioral dysfunction, CBT aims to identify and challenge negative cognitions while promoting adaptive coping strategies and problem-solving skills. Through structured interventions such as cognitive restructuring, exposure therapy, and behavioral activation, CBT empowers individuals to break free from cycles of rumination, avoidance, and self-defeating behaviors, fostering resilience and promoting long-term recovery.

Eye movement desensitization and reprocessing (EMDR) offers a novel and integrative approach to trauma treatment, combining elements of cognitive-behavioral therapy with bilateral stimulation techniques to facilitate the processing and integration of traumatic memories. Grounded in the adaptive information processing model, EMDR posits that traumatic experiences become maladaptively stored in memory networks, leading to symptoms such as flashbacks, hypervigilance, and emotional dysregulation. By engaging in rhythmic bilateral stimulation, such as eye movements or tactile sensations, individuals can access and reprocess traumatic memories, allowing for the resolution of emotional distress and the restoration of adaptive functioning.

Dialectical behavior therapy (DBT), originally developed to treat individuals with borderline personality disorder, has emerged as a highly effective intervention for trauma-related symptoms and emotion dysregulation. Combining elements of cognitive-behavioral therapy, mindfulness, and dialectical philosophy, DBT emphasizes acceptance, validation, and skill-building to enhance emotional resilience and interpersonal effectiveness. Through a structured curriculum of individual therapy, skills training groups, phone coaching, and consultation teams, DBT equips individuals with practical tools for distress tolerance, emotion regulation, interpersonal effectiveness, and mindfulness, fostering a sense of empowerment and agency in navigating life's challenges.

In summary, the transition to evidence-based approaches represents a watershed moment in the field of trauma treatment, heralding a departure from untested or speculative interventions toward scientifically validated methodologies with demonstrated efficacy. Cognitive-behavioral therapy, eye movement desensitization and reprocessing, and dialectical behavior therapy exemplify the evolution of trauma treatment, offering innovative and empirically supported interventions that prioritize symptom reduction, functional improvement, and long-term recovery. By embracing evidence-based practice, clinicians and researchers can continue to advance the field of trauma treatment, offering hope and healing to individuals grappling with the enduring effects of psychological trauma.

Trauma-Informed Care

Trauma-informed care represents a transformative paradigm shift in the provision of services across diverse settings, recognizing the widespread prevalence and profound impact of trauma on individuals' lives. Whether in healthcare, education, social services, or other contexts, trauma-informed approaches prioritize safety, trustworthiness, choice, collaboration, and empowerment, aiming to create environments that foster healing and resilience. At the core of trauma-informed care is the recognition that trauma is pervasive and often invisible, necessitating a sensitive and compassionate response that respects the dignity and autonomy of survivors.

In healthcare settings, trauma-informed care entails creating environments that prioritize physical and emotional safety and recognizing the potential triggers and vulnerabilities of trauma survivors. This may involve implementing trauma screening protocols, providing trauma-informed training for healthcare providers, and offering trauma-specific interventions such as trauma-focused therapy or mindfulness-based stress reduction. By cultivating a culture of safety, trust, and collaboration, healthcare organizations can enhance the quality of care and improve outcomes for trauma survivors across the lifespan.

In educational settings, trauma-informed approaches seek to create supportive learning environments that accommodate the diverse needs and experiences of students impacted by trauma. Educators and school personnel receive training on trauma awareness and sensitivity, equipping them with strategies for recognizing and responding to trauma-related behaviors in the classroom. Additionally, schools may implement trauma-informed practices such as trauma-sensitive curricula, restorative justice approaches, and supportive counseling services to promote academic success and social-emotional well-being for all students.

Within social services agencies, trauma-informed care emphasizes the importance of building trusting and collaborative relationships with clients, recognizing their strengths, resilience, and capacity for self-determination. This may involve adopting trauma-informed assessment tools, providing trauma-specific interventions such as trauma-focused cognitive-behavioral therapy or dialectical behavior therapy, and offering trauma-sensitive case management services that prioritize client choice and autonomy. By centering the needs and preferences of trauma survivors, social services agencies can empower individuals to navigate complex systems and access resources that promote healing and recovery.

Moreover, trauma-informed care extends beyond individual interactions to encompass broader systemic changes that address the root causes of trauma and promote social justice and equity. This may involve advocating for policy reforms, supporting trauma-informed legislation, and collaborating with community stakeholders to create trauma-responsive systems and services that address the intersecting needs of diverse populations. By addressing the underlying determinants of trauma, including poverty, discrimination, and systemic oppression, trauma-informed care seeks to create a more just and compassionate society where all individuals can thrive and flourish.

Advances in Neuroscience

Advances in neuroscience have revolutionized our understanding of trauma and its treatment, offering unprecedented insights into the neural mechanisms underlying the development and maintenance of trauma-related symptoms. Through techniques such as functional magnetic resonance imaging (fMRI), electroencephalography (EEG), and positron emission tomography (PET), researchers have uncovered distinct patterns of brain activity and connectivity associated with trauma exposure, shedding light on the intricate interplay between neural pathways, cognitive processes, and emotional regulation. This neurobiological perspective has paved the way for innovative interventions that target specific neural circuits and mechanisms implicated in trauma-related psychopathology, offering new avenues for healing and recovery.

One such intervention is neurofeedback, a form of biofeedback that enables individuals to modulate their brain activity in real-time through visual or auditory feedback. By monitoring neural activity using EEG or fMRI technology, neurofeedback allows individuals to learn to regulate patterns of brain activity associated with trauma-related symptoms such as hyperarousal, dissociation, or emotional dysregulation. Through repeated practice and reinforcement, individuals can develop greater control over their brain functioning, reducing the intensity and frequency of trauma-related symptoms and promoting adaptive coping strategies.

Mindfulness-based therapies represent another promising approach to trauma treatment, drawing upon principles of mindfulness meditation to cultivate present-moment awareness, acceptance, and nonjudgmental observation of thoughts and emotions. Research suggests that mindfulness practices can modulate neural activity in regions implicated in emotion regulation, attentional control, and self-awareness, offering potential therapeutic benefits for trauma survivors. Mindfulness-based interventions such as mindfulness-based stress reduction (MBSR) and mindfulness-based cognitive therapy (MBCT) have been shown to reduce symptoms of PTSD, depression, and anxiety, promoting greater resilience and well-being.

Furthermore, advances in neuroscience have informed the development of trauma-focused therapies such as eye movement desensitization and reprocessing (EMDR) and cognitive processing therapy (CPT), which target specific neural pathways involved in memory processing, fear extinction, and cognitive restructuring. EMDR, for example, incorporates bilateral stimulation techniques to facilitate the reprocessing and integration of traumatic memories, harnessing the brain's natural capacity for adaptive information processing. Similarly, CPT utilizes cognitive restructuring techniques to challenge maladaptive beliefs and schemas associated with trauma, promoting cognitive flexibility and emotional resilience.

In summary, advances in neuroscience have revolutionized our understanding of trauma and its treatment, offering novel insights into the neurobiological underpinnings of trauma-related psychopathology. By targeting specific neural pathways and mechanisms implicated in trauma, interventions such as neurofeedback, mindfulness-based therapies, and trauma-focused therapies offer new hope for healing and recovery. By harnessing the brain's innate capacity for adaptation and plasticity, these interventions empower individuals to transcend the legacy of trauma and reclaim agency, meaning, and vitality in their lives.

In the journey through understanding trauma, we've delved into the depths of human experience, where the heart-wrenching impact of overwhelming events leaves scars both seen and unseen. Trauma isn't just an event; it's a shattering of the soul, an upheaval that reverberates through our very being.

From defining trauma as the storm that overwhelms our shores to unraveling its nuanced effects on the mind and body, we've witnessed the intricate dance between our biology and the world around us. Our brains, intricate bonds of memory and emotion, bear the imprint of trauma, rewired by the forces that seek to break us.

But among the darkness, there is light. Through the annals of time, we've seen the evolution of trauma treatment, from the crude tools of ancient healers to the precise interventions of modern science. We've witnessed the shift from ignorance to enlightenment, from superstition to evidence-based practice.

Yet, perhaps the most profound revelation lies not in the methods we employ but in the compassion with which we wield them. Trauma-informed care isn't just a set of techniques; it's a philosophy— a recognition of our shared humanity and the profound impact of our actions on one another.

As we stand at the crossroads of history and healing, let us remember that trauma isn't just a clinical diagnosis; it's a human experience. It's the silent cries in the night, the trembling hands reaching out for solace, the resilience that refuses to be broken.

In our journey forward, may we carry with us the wisdom of ages past and the promise of a brighter tomorrow. And may we, in our words and deeds, offer not just treatment but hope—a beacon of light in the darkest of nights. In the end, it is not just the trauma we endure that defines us, but the courage with which we rise above it.

Chapter Three
The Brain on Trauma

When an individual experiences trauma, whether it's a single acute event or ongoing exposure to stressors, the brain initiates an immediate response to cope with the perceived threat. This response involves activation of the stress response system, which is orchestrated by a complex interplay of neural and hormonal pathways. One key aspect of this response is the release of stress hormones like cortisol and adrenaline from the adrenal glands. These hormones flood the bloodstream, preparing the body to react swiftly to the danger at hand. Cortisol, often termed the "stress hormone," mobilizes energy reserves by increasing blood sugar levels, while adrenaline enhances arousal and alertness, facilitating a rapid response to potential threats.

Changes in brain structure resulting from trauma can have profound implications for various aspects of cognitive and emotional functioning. One notable area affected is emotion regulation, where alterations in brain regions involved in processing and regulating emotions, such as the amygdala and prefrontal cortex, can lead to difficulties in effectively managing emotional responses. For instance, trauma-induced changes in the amygdala may result in heightened emotional reactivity, making individuals more susceptible to experiencing intense and uncontrollable emotions. Similarly, disruptions in the prefrontal cortex, which is responsible for inhibiting emotional responses and exerting cognitive control, can lead to impulsivity and difficulty in regulating emotions in a flexible and adaptive manner.

Furthermore, trauma-related alterations in brain structure can impact memory consolidation processes, affecting the encoding and retrieval of memories, particularly those associated with the traumatic event. The hippocampus, a region critical for memory formation, may undergo changes in volume and connectivity following trauma, leading to impairments in the consolidation and retrieval of traumatic memories. This can result in fragmented or distorted memory recall, contributing to symptoms such as flashbacks and intrusive memories characteristic of post-traumatic stress disorder (PTSD).

Moreover, trauma-induced changes in neural circuits can increase susceptibility to mental health disorders such as depression and anxiety. Dysregulation in stress-responsive pathways, including the hypothalamic-pituitary-adrenal (HPA) axis and the limbic system, may contribute to chronic hyperarousal and heightened vulnerability to mood disorders. For example, alterations in neurotransmitter systems, such as serotonin and dopamine, implicated in mood regulation may exacerbate symptoms of depression and anxiety in individuals with a history of trauma.

Illustrating the diverse impact of trauma on brain structure and function across individuals and populations can provide valuable insights into the complexity of trauma-related outcomes. For instance, studies have shown that the effects of trauma can vary depending on factors such as the nature of the traumatic event, the age at which it occurred, and individual differences in resilience and coping mechanisms. Case studies and examples can highlight the wide range of responses to trauma, from resilience and adaptation to maladaptive coping strategies and the development of psychiatric disorders.

For example, while some individuals may exhibit resilience and minimal long-term effects on brain structure and function following trauma, others may experience significant difficulties in various cognitive and emotional domains. Furthermore, examining how trauma impacts brain structure and function across different populations, such as survivors of natural disasters, combat veterans, and individuals exposed to childhood abuse, can provide valuable insights into the unique challenges and vulnerabilities faced by diverse groups in the aftermath of trauma. Overall, recognizing the multifaceted nature of trauma's impact on the brain can inform more targeted interventions and support services tailored to the specific needs of trauma survivors.

Insights from Neuroscience

Neurobiological Mechanisms

Neuroscience research has made significant strides in elucidating the neurobiological mechanisms underlying the response to trauma, shedding light on how the brain processes and adapts to traumatic experiences. One key finding is the involvement of the stress response system, which encompasses a complex interplay of neurotransmitters, neuroendocrine systems, and neural circuits. In response to trauma, the amygdala, often referred to as the brain's fear center, quickly assesses the threat and activates the hypothalamus, triggering the release of stress hormones like cortisol and adrenaline. These hormones prepare the body to respond to the threat by mobilizing energy reserves and enhancing arousal and alertness.

Furthermore, neurotransmitters such as serotonin, dopamine, and norepinephrine play crucial roles in modulating mood, arousal, and stress responses. Dysregulation in these neurotransmitter systems has been implicated in the development and maintenance of trauma-related disorders such as post-traumatic stress disorder (PTSD), depression, and anxiety. For example, alterations in serotonin signaling have been associated with mood disturbances and emotional dysregulation in individuals with a history of trauma. Similarly, abnormalities in dopamine and norepinephrine function may contribute to symptoms of hyperarousal and hypervigilance characteristic of PTSD.

Advances in neuroimaging techniques have revolutionized our understanding of the neural basis of trauma-related disorders by allowing researchers to visualize and quantify structural and functional changes in the brain. Techniques such as functional magnetic resonance imaging (fMRI), positron emission tomography (PET), and diffusion tensor imaging (DTI) have provided insights into the alterations in neural circuits implicated in stress response, emotion regulation, and memory processing following trauma exposure. For example, neuroimaging studies have revealed abnormalities in the amygdala, hippocampus, and prefrontal cortex in individuals with PTSD, highlighting the role of these brain regions in the pathophysiology of the disorder.

Moreover, molecular neuroscience approaches have deepened our understanding of the cellular and molecular mechanisms underlying trauma response, offering potential targets for pharmacological interventions. Researchers have identified changes in gene expression, synaptic plasticity, and neuroinflammation associated with trauma exposure, providing insights into the long-term effects of trauma on brain function and structure. By elucidating the intricate mechanisms through which trauma alters brain function, molecular neuroscience holds promise for the development of novel therapeutic strategies aimed at mitigating the impact of trauma-related disorders and promoting recovery and resilience. Overall, the integration of neurobiological findings from various disciplines has advanced our understanding of the neural basis of trauma response and holds promise for improving clinical outcomes for individuals affected by trauma.

Biological Vulnerabilities

Genetic and epigenetic factors play critical roles in shaping individual vulnerability or resilience in response to trauma. Genetic factors refer to variations in DNA sequence that can influence an individual's susceptibility to trauma-related disorders. Research has identified several genetic polymorphisms associated with increased risk for conditions such as post-traumatic stress disorder (PTSD), depression, and anxiety following trauma exposure. For example, variations in genes encoding for neurotransmitter receptors, such as the serotonin transporter gene (SLC6A4), have been linked to differences in emotional regulation and stress responsiveness.

In addition to genetic factors, epigenetic mechanisms regulate gene expression in response to environmental influences, including trauma. Epigenetic modifications, such as DNA methylation and histone acetylation, can alter the expression of genes involved in stress response and emotion regulation, thereby influencing an individual's vulnerability or resilience to trauma-related disorders. For instance, studies have shown that early-life adversity can lead to epigenetic changes in genes associated with the hypothalamic-pituitary-adrenal (HPA) axis and the stress response system, increasing susceptibility to psychiatric disorders later in life.

Furthermore, gene-environment interactions play a crucial role in determining individual differences in susceptibility to trauma-related disorders. Genetic predispositions may interact with environmental factors, such as exposure to trauma or social support, to shape an individual's response to stress and adversity. For example, individuals with a genetic predisposition for heightened stress reactivity may be more susceptible to developing PTSD following trauma exposure, particularly in the absence of adequate social support or coping resources.

Developmental factors, such as early-life adversity and childhood trauma, can have profound and lasting effects on brain development and mental health outcomes. Adverse experiences during critical periods of brain development can disrupt the formation of neural circuits involved in emotion regulation, stress response, and cognitive functioning. Moreover, childhood trauma has been associated with alterations in brain structure and function, including changes in the volume of brain regions such as the amygdala, hippocampus, and prefrontal cortex.

Overall, understanding the complex interplay between genetic, epigenetic, and developmental factors is essential for elucidating the mechanisms underlying vulnerability and resilience to trauma-related disorders. By identifying genetic and epigenetic markers associated with increased risk for psychiatric disorders following trauma exposure, researchers can develop more personalized interventions aimed at mitigating the impact of trauma and promoting recovery and resilience. Additionally, interventions targeting developmental factors, such as early intervention programs and trauma-informed care, can help mitigate the long-term effects of childhood trauma on brain development and mental health outcomes.

The Brain's Adaptability and Potential for Recovery

Neuroplasticity and Resilience

Neuroplasticity is a fundamental concept in neuroscience that refers to the brain's remarkable ability to adapt and reorganize in response to experiences, including trauma. This concept challenges the traditional view of the brain as a static organ and highlights its dynamic nature, with neural circuits constantly reshaping themselves based on activity and experience. Understanding neuroplasticity is crucial for comprehending the brain's capacity for adaptation and recovery following trauma, as it underscores the brain's potential for change and growth even in the face of adversity.

Research findings have demonstrated the brain's remarkable ability to reorganize neural circuits, form new connections, and recover function in response to supportive environments and interventions. Neuroimaging studies have revealed structural and functional changes in the brain following trauma exposure, including alterations in the size, connectivity, and activity of brain regions implicated in emotion regulation, memory processing, and stress response. Moreover, studies in animal models and human populations have shown that environmental enrichment, social support, and psychological interventions can promote neuroplasticity and facilitate recovery from trauma-related symptoms.

Factors that promote resilience play a critical role in fostering adaptive neuroplasticity and facilitating recovery following trauma. Social support, including relationships with family, friends, and community, can provide a buffer against the negative effects of trauma and promote adaptive coping strategies. Moreover, individuals who possess effective coping strategies, such as problem-solving skills, emotional regulation techniques, and mindfulness practices, may be better equipped to navigate the challenges associated with trauma and promote neuroplasticity.

Psychological interventions aimed at fostering adaptive neuroplasticity can also play a crucial role in promoting resilience and facilitating recovery following trauma. Therapeutic approaches such as cognitive-behavioral therapy (CBT), eye movement desensitization and reprocessing (EMDR), and mindfulness-based interventions have been shown to promote neuroplasticity and facilitate recovery from trauma-related symptoms. These interventions aim to modify maladaptive patterns of thinking and behavior, promote emotional regulation, and enhance coping skills, thereby promoting adaptive neuroplasticity and facilitating recovery from trauma-related disorders.

Understanding the concept of neuroplasticity is essential for understanding the brain's capacity for adaptation and recovery following trauma. By exploring research findings on the brain's ability to reorganize neural circuits and form new connections, discussing factors that promote resilience, and highlighting the role of psychological interventions in fostering adaptive neuroplasticity, we can gain insights into effective strategies for promoting recovery and resilience in individuals affected by trauma. Ultimately, recognizing the brain's capacity for change and growth underscores the importance of early intervention and support in helping individuals recover from traumatic experiences and regain a sense of well-being.

Therapeutic Interventions

Evidence-based interventions for addressing trauma-related symptoms and promoting recovery encompass a variety of therapeutic modalities. Trauma-focused cognitive-behavioral therapy (CBT) is one of the most widely researched and effective treatments for trauma survivors. This approach involves helping individuals identify and challenge maladaptive beliefs and behaviors related to the traumatic event while also providing coping strategies to manage distressing symptoms. Through gradual exposure to trauma-related memories and situations, individuals can learn to process and integrate their experiences in a safe and supportive environment.

Eye movement desensitization and reprocessing (EMDR) is another evidence-based intervention that has shown efficacy in treating trauma-related symptoms. EMDR involves a structured protocol where individuals recall distressing memories while simultaneously engaging in bilateral stimulation, such as eye movements or tapping. This process is thought to facilitate the reprocessing of traumatic memories, allowing individuals to integrate the experiences in a less distressing manner. EMDR has been found to reduce symptoms of PTSD and improve overall functioning in trauma survivors.

Mindfulness-based approaches, such as mindfulness-based stress reduction (MBSR) and mindfulness-based cognitive therapy (MBCT), have also demonstrated effectiveness in reducing trauma-related symptoms. These interventions teach individuals to cultivate present-moment awareness and acceptance of their thoughts, emotions, and bodily sensations. By developing mindfulness skills, individuals can learn to approach their traumatic memories and emotions with greater equanimity, reducing the impact of distressing symptoms on their daily functioning.

In addition to psychotherapeutic interventions, pharmacological treatments targeting neurobiological mechanisms implicated in trauma response can be an important component of trauma treatment. Selective serotonin reuptake inhibitors (SSRIs) are commonly prescribed medications that have been shown to reduce symptoms of depression and anxiety in trauma survivors. Other psychotropic medications, such as antipsychotics and mood stabilizers, may also be used to target specific symptoms, such as dissociation or agitation.

Integrated and multidisciplinary approaches to trauma treatment are essential for addressing the complex interplay between biological, psychological, and social factors involved in trauma response. By combining biological interventions, such as pharmacotherapy, with psychosocial interventions, such as therapy and support groups, individuals can receive comprehensive and holistic care that addresses their unique needs. Moreover, incorporating complementary approaches, such as yoga, art therapy, or animal-assisted therapy, can provide additional avenues for healing and recovery. By recognizing the multifaceted nature of trauma and tailoring treatment approaches to individual needs, clinicians can maximize the likelihood of positive outcomes and long-term recovery for trauma survivors.

Hope and Healing

Ultimately, it is crucial to stress that even while trauma has far-reaching effects, there is always a chance for healing and development. Even after experiencing a traumatic event, the human brain is very resilient and adaptable. Healing is a process, not a destination; it's not impossible, and with the right people by your side and the tools you need, you can get back on your feet. Trauma survivors may find hope and strength in the realization that they are more than their experiences and that a better future is possible when we recognize the brain's capacity for development and evolution.

One powerful source of hope lies in the stories of resilience and transformation demonstrated by individuals who have overcome trauma. These stories serve as a testament to the human spirit's ability to triumph over adversity and find meaning, purpose, and connection in the face of unimaginable challenges. Whether it's a survivor of childhood abuse who finds strength in advocating for others, a veteran who rebuilds their life after combat trauma, or a community coming together to support one another in the aftermath of a natural disaster, these stories inspire hope and remind us of the inherent resilience within each of us.

In addition to stories of resilience, providing practical resources and recommendations for further support and self-care is essential for empowering readers to take proactive steps towards healing and recovery. This may include information on trauma-informed therapy options, support groups, hotlines, and online resources where individuals can access guidance, information, and support. Additionally, self-care practices such as mindfulness meditation, exercise, creative expression, and connecting with supportive relationships can play a crucial role in promoting healing and well-being. By equipping readers with the tools and resources they need to prioritize their mental and emotional health, we empower them to take ownership of their healing journey and cultivate a sense of agency and resilience.

While trauma may leave scars, it does not define who we are or determine our future. By fostering a message of hope, sharing stories of resilience, and providing practical resources for support and self-care, we can inspire individuals to embrace their inner strength, cultivate resilience, and embark on a journey toward healing and recovery. Together, we can create a supportive and compassionate community where survivors feel empowered to heal, grow, and thrive in the aftermath of trauma.

Chapter Four
The Body's Memory

Keeping the Score

Exploring the complex connection between psychological trauma and somatic sensations, the idea that the body may hold memories and experiences even when the mind can't consciously remember them is explored. It is very uncommon for people who have gone through traumatic experiences to deal with ongoing mental and physical symptoms that they cannot put their finger on. This phenomenon shows how trauma affects the whole body and undermines the idea that memory is only in the brain.

A complicated web of neurons, hormones, and physiological reactions forms the basis of the human experience, which in turn forms the basis of the body's memory storage capacity. The body goes through a series of reactions meant to keep you alive when you're threatened or when anything unpleasant happens. The neurological system encodes these reactions to help in adaptation and protection. This adaptation mechanism is normally well-regulated in the body, but it may become dysregulated in the aftermath of severe trauma, causing memories to get embedded in the muscles and cells.

New insights into the workings of body memory have emerged from studies in psychology and neuroscience. According to studies, the way information is processed and stored may be altered by alterations in brain structure and function that might be induced by traumatic events. Encoding and consolidation of traumatic memories are also influenced by the body's stress response system, which includes the production of chemicals like adrenaline and cortisol. Because of this physiological imprinting, the body can detect danger even when the mind isn't actively involved.

Additionally, the idea that the body is always "keeping the score" encompasses a vast array of physical feelings and experiences, going beyond conventional ideas of memory. Reminders of traumatic experiences may manifest in a variety of ways, including physical symptoms, ongoing physical discomfort, or unexplained emotional responses. People who have experienced trauma often express physical symptoms, including headaches, muscular tension, and gastrointestinal issues, which further emphasizes the connection between the mind and body.

Essentially, the idea that our bodies can hold memories provides a deep understanding of how the human experience is interconnected. Healing and rehabilitation may be approached from a more holistic perspective when both patients and practitioners recognize the importance of the body in storing and expressing trauma. By using trauma-informed treatment, mindfulness techniques, somatic therapy, and other similar approaches, one may address the long-lasting effects of traumatic events and promote physical and mental recovery.

Origins of The Term

The term "keeping the score" in the context of the body retaining memories of trauma originated from the groundbreaking work of Dr. Bessel van der Kolk, a prominent psychiatrist and researcher in the field of trauma and PTSD. In his seminal book " The Body Keeps the Score," Dr. van der Kolk explores the profound impact of trauma on both the mind and body, challenging conventional views of psychological disorders as purely cognitive or emotional phenomena. Drawing from decades of clinical experience and scientific research, he offers insights into how traumatic experiences become imprinted within the body's cellular and physiological systems.

Dr. van der Kolk's exploration into the origins of the term traces back to his observations of patients grappling with the enduring effects of trauma. Through his clinical practice, he encountered numerous individuals whose experiences of distress, disconnection, and physical ailments seemed inexplicably intertwined with past traumatic events. These observations led him to theorize that traumatic memories are not only stored in the brain but also manifested somatically within the body's nervous, endocrine, and immune systems.

The concept of the body "keeping the score" underscores the interconnectedness of psychological and physiological processes in the experience and expression of trauma. Dr. van der Kolk elucidates how traumatic experiences can disrupt the body's natural rhythms and regulatory mechanisms, leading to a myriad of symptoms ranging from chronic pain and somatic complaints to mood disturbances and dissociative states. By reframing trauma as a whole-body experience, he advocates for holistic approaches to healing that address the underlying physiological imprints of past trauma.

Furthermore, Dr. van der Kolk's work highlights the limitations of traditional psychotherapeutic approaches in adequately addressing the complex needs of trauma survivors. He emphasizes the importance of incorporating body-centered interventions such as yoga, mindfulness, and somatic experiencing into treatment modalities to facilitate healing on both psychological and physiological levels. Through these approaches, individuals are empowered to reconnect with their bodies, reclaim a sense of agency, and integrate fragmented aspects of their selves that have been fragmented by trauma.

In essence, the origins of the term "keeping the score" underscore a paradigm shift in our understanding of trauma and its effects on the human experience. Dr. van der Kolk's pioneering work continues to inform and inspire researchers, clinicians, and individuals alike, offering hope for a more compassionate and effective approach to healing from trauma. By recognizing the intricate interplay between mind and body, we can cultivate greater resilience, restore wholeness, and embark on a journey towards recovery and transformation.

Understanding Somatic Experiencing

Understanding somatic experiences delves into the profound notion that trauma is not solely confined to the realm of the mind but is deeply ingrained within the body's physiological responses. Developed by Dr. Peter A. Levine, somatic experiencing is a therapeutic approach that acknowledges the somatic manifestations of trauma and seeks to facilitate healing through the exploration and regulation of bodily sensations. This framework posits that traumatic experiences, whether acute or chronic, can disrupt the body's natural capacity to process and release stress, leading to the accumulation of unresolved tension and dysregulation within the nervous system.

Central to the concept of somatic experiencing is the understanding that trauma is stored in the body and can manifest in a variety of physical symptoms, emotions, and behaviors. When an individual experiences a traumatic event, the body's innate survival mechanisms, such as the fight, flight, or freeze response, are activated to cope with the perceived threat. However, in cases where the threat is overwhelming or prolonged, the body may become stuck in a state of hyperarousal or hyperarousal, resulting in a range of somatic disturbances.

These somatic disturbances may manifest as chronic pain, tension, or discomfort in various parts of the body, reflecting the physiological imprint of past trauma. Additionally, emotional dysregulation, such as anxiety, depression, or heightened arousal, may arise as the body attempts to cope with the unresolved stress and tension stored within its tissues. Behaviors such as avoidance, numbing, or self-destructive tendencies can further perpetuate the cycle of trauma, creating barriers to healing and integration.

Through somatic experiencing, individuals are guided to explore and renegotiate their relationship with bodily sensations, emotions, and impulses in a safe and supportive therapeutic environment. By attuning to the body's innate wisdom and resilience, individuals can gradually release stored tension, discharge pent-up energy, and restore a sense of balance and vitality. Through gentle yet profound interventions, such as breathwork, mindful movement, and tracking bodily sensations, somatic experiencing offers a pathway to healing that honors the interconnectedness of mind, body, and spirit.

The understanding of somatic experiencing illuminates the intricate interplay between trauma and the body's physiological responses, offering a holistic framework for healing and transformation. By embracing the wisdom of the body and cultivating compassionate awareness, individuals can reclaim agency over their experiences, restore equilibrium, and embark on a journey toward wholeness and resilience.

Examples of Body Memory

Examples of body memory offer compelling insights into the profound ways in which trauma can become encoded within the somatic experience of individuals. These anecdotes and case studies serve as poignant reminders of the enduring impact of past traumatic events on the body's physiology, emotions, and behaviors. One notable example is that of a combat veteran who, upon hearing a sudden loud noise resembling gunfire, experiences an immediate surge of adrenaline and hypervigilance, even in the absence of any real threat. This visceral reaction reflects the body's ingrained response to past trauma, wherein sensory triggers evoke intense physiological responses linked to the traumatic memory.

Similarly, survivors of physical or sexual assault may experience intrusive sensations or pain in areas of the body associated with the trauma. For instance, a survivor of sexual abuse may report feeling a tightening sensation in their chest or abdomen when confronted with reminders of the traumatic event. These somatic responses serve as visceral reminders of the trauma, often surfacing unexpectedly and disrupting the individual's sense of safety and well-being. Through the lens of body memory, these physical sensations are understood as manifestations of the unresolved tension and dysregulation stored within the body's cellular and muscular systems.

Furthermore, individuals who have experienced traumatic accidents or injuries may exhibit symptoms of body memory in the form of chronic pain or somatic complaints. For instance, a car accident survivor may continue to experience persistent headaches or muscle tension long after the physical injuries have healed. Despite medical interventions and treatments, these somatic symptoms persist, reflecting the deeper imprint of trauma on the body's nervous system and physiology. In such cases, traditional approaches to pain management may prove insufficient, highlighting the importance of addressing the underlying psychological and somatic components of the individual's distress.

Moreover, individuals with a history of complex trauma, such as childhood abuse or neglect, may exhibit a wide range of somatic symptoms and emotional dysregulation linked to early developmental experiences. For example, an adult survivor of childhood trauma may struggle with digestive issues, insomnia, or chronic fatigue, all of which are commonly associated with the long-term effects of early relational trauma. Through therapeutic interventions that address the somatic manifestations of trauma, individuals can begin to unravel the complex web of physical and emotional distress, reclaiming a sense of agency and empowerment in their healing journey.

Examples of body memory underscore the interconnectedness of trauma and the somatic experience, highlighting the enduring impact of past events on the body's physiology and functioning. By acknowledging and validating these somatic responses, individuals can cultivate greater self-awareness and compassion, paving the way for healing and integration on both psychological and physiological levels. Through trauma-informed care and holistic therapeutic approaches, individuals can embark on a journey towards reclaiming agency over their bodies and restoring a sense of wholeness and well-being.

Physiological Responses to Trauma

Fight, Flight, Or Freeze Response

The fight, flight, or freeze response is a primal survival mechanism ingrained within the human nervous system, designed to mobilize the body's resources in the face of perceived threats. When confronted with danger, the body undergoes a cascade of physiological changes aimed at increasing its chances of survival. In the "fight" response, individuals may experience heightened arousal and aggression, preparing to confront the threat head-on. Conversely, the "flight" response triggers a surge of adrenaline and the urge to flee from the perceived danger. In situations where neither fighting nor fleeing is feasible, the body may enter a state of "freeze," characterized by immobilization and dissociation as a means of self-preservation.

However, trauma can profoundly dysregulate these instinctual responses, leading to a range of maladaptive coping mechanisms and physiological disturbances. For individuals who have experienced overwhelming or repeated trauma, the fight, flight, or freeze response may become hyperactive or chronically activated, even in the absence of real threats. This chronic state of hyperarousal can manifest as heightened anxiety, hypervigilance, or aggression, making it difficult for individuals to regulate their emotions and behaviors in everyday situations.

Conversely, trauma can also lead to dysregulation of the freeze response, wherein individuals may become stuck in a state of immobilization or dissociation in the face of perceived threats. This may manifest as a numbing of emotions, feelings of detachment from oneself or one's surroundings, or a sense of being overwhelmed and unable to respond effectively to stressors. In extreme cases, chronic freeze responses can contribute to the development of conditions such as dissociative disorders or complex PTSD, further exacerbating the individual's sense of disconnection and distress.

Also, the dysregulation of the fight, flight, or freeze response can have profound implications for both physical and mental health. Chronic activation of the stress response system, including the release of stress hormones such as cortisol and adrenaline, can contribute to a range of health problems, including cardiovascular disease, immune dysfunction, and digestive disorders. Additionally, the constant state of arousal or shutdown can take a toll on the individual's psychological well-being, leading to symptoms of anxiety, depression, and post-traumatic stress disorder (PTSD).

The fight, flight, or freeze response illustrates the complex interplay between the body and mind in responding to perceived threats. While these instinctual reactions are vital for survival, trauma can disrupt the delicate balance of the nervous system, leading to dysregulation and maladaptive responses. By recognizing and addressing the underlying physiological and psychological factors contributing to these disturbances, individuals can begin to restore a sense of safety, agency, and resilience in the face of adversity.

Stress Hormones

Trauma, whether experienced as a single acute event or chronic adversity, triggers a profound physiological response known as the stress response. Central to this response is the release of stress hormones, including cortisol and adrenaline, which orchestrate the body's adaptive reactions to perceived threats. When an individual encounters a traumatic event, the brain's amygdala, a key center for processing emotions, sends distress signals to the hypothalamus, prompting the activation of the body's stress axis, known as the hypothalamic-pituitary-adrenal (HPA) axis.

Upon activation of the HPA axis, the hypothalamus releases corticotropin-releasing hormone (CRH), which signals the pituitary gland to produce adrenocorticotropic hormone (ACTH). ACTH then stimulates the adrenal glands, located atop the kidneys, to release cortisol and adrenaline into the bloodstream. These stress hormones mobilize the body's resources, increasing heart rate, blood pressure, and glucose levels to prepare for action. In the short term, this physiological response is adaptive, enhancing the individual's chances of survival in the face of immediate danger.

However, in cases of chronic or repeated trauma, the prolonged activation of the stress response system can have profound and lasting effects on the body's physiology and functioning. Elevated levels of cortisol, often referred to as the "stress hormone," can disrupt the body's natural rhythms and regulatory mechanisms, leading to a range of health problems. Chronic exposure to high levels of cortisol has been associated with an increased risk of cardiovascular disease, immune suppression, metabolic disorders, and cognitive impairments.

Likewise, adrenaline, also known as epinephrine, plays a key role in mobilizing the body's energy reserves during times of stress. However, excessive or prolonged release of adrenaline can contribute to symptoms of anxiety, hyperarousal, and sleep disturbances. Moreover, both cortisol and adrenaline have been implicated in the development and maintenance of mental health disorders such as anxiety disorders, depression, and post-traumatic stress disorder (PTSD), further highlighting the intricate interplay between trauma, stress hormones, and psychological well-being.

Trauma activates the release of stress hormones such as cortisol and adrenaline as part of the body's adaptive response to perceived threats. While this response is essential for survival in the short term, chronic or repeated trauma can dysregulate the stress response system, leading to a cascade of physiological and psychological disturbances. By understanding the complex interplay between trauma and stress hormones, individuals and practitioners alike can adopt more comprehensive approaches to healing and recovery, addressing both the psychological and physiological dimensions of trauma-related distress.

Impact on The Nervous System

Traumatic experiences can have a profound impact on the nervous system, disrupting its delicate balance and functionality. One common consequence of trauma is the dysregulation of the autonomic nervous system (ANS), which controls automatic bodily functions such as heart rate, digestion, and respiratory rate. Trauma can overwhelm the ANS, leading to two distinct states of arousal: chronic hyperarousal and hyperarousal. In a state of chronic hyperarousal, individuals may experience heightened sensitivity to environmental stimuli, leading to hypervigilance, anxiety, and exaggerated startle responses. This heightened state of alertness is fueled by the constant activation of the sympathetic nervous system, the branch of the ANS responsible for the "fight or flight" response.

Conversely, trauma can also lead to states of chronic hyperarousal, wherein individuals exhibit a diminished capacity for emotional and physiological responsiveness. This state of dissociation or shutdown is characterized by a numbing of emotions, reduced sensory perception, and feelings of detachment from oneself or one's surroundings. Chronic hyperarousal is often associated with the dominance of the parasympathetic nervous system, which governs rest, relaxation, and conservation of energy. In cases of severe trauma or repeated exposure to adversity, individuals may enter a state of dissociative immobilization, wherein the body's natural instincts for self-protection are overridden by a profound sense of helplessness and resignation.

The impact of trauma on the nervous system extends beyond acute stress responses, influencing the structure and function of key brain regions involved in emotion regulation, memory processing, and threat detection. Chronic hyperarousal and hyperarousal can lead to alterations in the amygdala, the hippocampus, and the prefrontal cortex, among other areas. These changes may contribute to symptoms of anxiety, depression, and post-traumatic stress disorder (PTSD), further exacerbating the individual's sense of distress and dysfunction.

Moreover, the dysregulation of the nervous system can have far-reaching effects on both physical and mental health. Chronic hyperarousal is associated with an increased risk of cardiovascular disease, immune dysfunction, and metabolic disorders, while chronic hyperarousal may lead to symptoms of chronic fatigue, digestive disturbances, and chronic pain. Furthermore, the dysregulation of the nervous system can interfere with interpersonal relationships, work performance, and overall quality of life, perpetuating a cycle of distress and dysfunction.

In essence, traumatic experiences can overwhelm the nervous system, leading to chronic hyperarousal or hyperarousal and disrupting the body's natural capacity for regulation and resilience. By understanding the impact of trauma on the nervous system, individuals and practitioners can adopt more comprehensive approaches to healing and recovery, addressing both the psychological and physiological dimensions of trauma-related distress. Through trauma-informed care, somatic experiencing techniques, and holistic interventions, individuals can begin to restore balance and vitality to their nervous systems, reclaiming a sense of agency and well-being in the process.

Dysfunctional Coping Mechanisms

In the wake of trauma, individuals may develop a myriad of maladaptive coping mechanisms as a means of managing overwhelming emotions, memories, and sensations. One such dysfunctional coping mechanism is substance abuse, wherein individuals turn to drugs or alcohol as a way to numb emotional pain, alleviate distressing symptoms, or escape from traumatic memories. Substance abuse provides temporary relief from the intense psychological and physiological distress associated with trauma, but it ultimately exacerbates the underlying issues and can lead to addiction, physical health problems, and social impairment. Moreover, substance abuse often serves as a form of self-medication, masking the symptoms of co-occurring mental health disorders such as anxiety, depression, and post-traumatic stress disorder (PTSD).

Another common maladaptive coping mechanism in response to trauma is self-harm, which encompasses a range of behaviors aimed at inflicting physical harm or injury to oneself. Self-harm may include cutting, burning, scratching, or hitting oneself as a way to cope with overwhelming emotions, regain a sense of control, or express inner turmoil. While self-harm may provide temporary relief from emotional pain, it ultimately perpetuates a cycle of self-destructive behavior and can lead to serious physical injuries, infections, and long-term consequences. Additionally, self-harm often co-occurs with other mental health disorders and may serve as a coping strategy for individuals struggling to regulate intense emotions or navigate interpersonal challenges.

Furthermore, individuals may resort to avoidance and withdrawal as coping mechanisms in response to trauma, avoiding reminders of the traumatic event or isolating themselves from others as a way to protect themselves from further distress. While avoidance may provide temporary relief from triggers and reminders of trauma, it ultimately perpetuates the cycle of avoidance and maintains the individual's sense of fear and vulnerability. Avoidance can lead to social isolation, interpersonal conflict, and difficulties in functioning at work, school, or in relationships. Moreover, avoidance may hinder the individual's ability to process and integrate the traumatic experience, prolonging their symptoms and impairing their recovery.

Additionally, dissociation is a common coping mechanism among individuals who have experienced trauma, wherein they disconnect from their thoughts, feelings, and sensations as a way to protect themselves from overwhelming distress. Dissociation may manifest as a sense of detachment from oneself or one's surroundings, memory gaps, or feelings of unreality. While dissociation may serve as a protective mechanism during traumatic events, chronic dissociation can interfere with daily functioning, memory consolidation, and sense of identity. Moreover, dissociation often co-occurs with other mental health disorders and may complicate the individual's ability to engage in therapy or other forms of treatment.

In essence, maladaptive coping mechanisms such as substance abuse, self-harm, avoidance, and dissociation are common responses to trauma, stemming from a need to manage overwhelming emotions, memories, and sensations. While these coping strategies may provide temporary relief from distress, they ultimately perpetuate the cycle of dysfunction and hinder the individual's ability to heal and recover from trauma. Through trauma-informed care, therapy, and support, individuals can learn healthier coping skills, address underlying issues, and embark on a journey toward healing and resilience.

The Role of the Nervous System

Introduction to The Nervous System

The nervous system serves as the command center of the human body, regulating and coordinating various physiological processes and responses to internal and external stimuli. It consists of two main components: the central nervous system (CNS) and the peripheral nervous system (PNS). The CNS, comprising the brain and spinal cord, is responsible for processing sensory information, initiating motor responses, and orchestrating complex cognitive functions. It serves as the hub of neural communication and integration, allowing for seamless coordination of bodily functions and behaviors.

The autonomic nervous system (ANS) is a crucial subdivision of the peripheral nervous system that regulates involuntary bodily functions, including heart rate, respiration, digestion, and glandular secretion. The ANS operates autonomously, meaning it functions independently of conscious control, allowing for the continuous monitoring and adjustment of internal physiological processes to maintain homeostasis. It consists of two main branches: the sympathetic nervous system (SNS) and the parasympathetic nervous system (PNS), each with distinct roles and functions.

The sympathetic nervous system (SNS) is often referred to as the "fight or flight" system, as it mobilizes the body's resources in response to perceived threats or stressors. When activated, the SNS triggers a series of physiological changes aimed at preparing the body for action, such as increasing heart rate, dilating pupils, and redirecting blood flow to the muscles. These adaptive responses enable individuals to respond quickly and effectively to danger, facilitating survival in threatening situations. However, chronic activation of the SNS can lead to symptoms of anxiety, hypertension, and other stress-related disorders.

Conversely, the parasympathetic nervous system (PNS) is responsible for promoting relaxation, rest, and digestion, often referred to as the "rest and digest" system. When activated, the PNS counteracts the effects of the SNS, restoring balance and conserving energy. It slows heart rate, constricts pupils, and stimulates digestion, allowing the body to recuperate and replenish its resources after periods of stress or activity. The PNS plays a crucial role in maintaining homeostasis and supporting the body's overall health and well-being.

In summary, the nervous system, comprised of the central nervous system (CNS) and the autonomic nervous system (ANS), governs a wide range of physiological processes and responses essential for survival and functioning. The ANS, with its sympathetic and parasympathetic branches, modulates involuntary bodily functions and regulates the body's response to stress and relaxation. Understanding the intricate workings of the nervous system provides valuable insights into the body's adaptive capabilities and the interconnectedness of physiological and psychological processes.

Polyvagal Theory

Stephen Porges' Polyvagal Theory offers a groundbreaking framework for understanding the complex interplay between the nervous system, emotions, and social behavior. At the core of this

Theory is the vagus nerve, a key component of the autonomic nervous system responsible for regulating visceral functions and influencing emotional and social responses. The vagus nerve comprises two main branches: the ventral vagus, associated with social engagement and relaxation, and the dorsal vagus, associated with immobilization and dissociation. Porges proposes that these two branches, along with the sympathetic nervous system, form a hierarchical system that orchestrates adaptive responses to environmental cues and threats.

One of the central tenets of Polyvagal Theory is the concept of neuroception, wherein the nervous system continuously evaluates environmental cues to assess safety and threat. Based on this assessment, the nervous system modulates physiological and behavioral responses to promote either social engagement or self-protection. In situations perceived as safe, the ventral vagus promotes social engagement, fostering feelings of connection, trust, and relaxation. Conversely, in situations perceived as threatening, the dorsal vagus and sympathetic nervous system initiate defensive responses such as immobilization, fight, flight, or freeze.

Polyvagal Theory has profound implications for understanding the body's response to trauma, as it sheds light on the physiological mechanisms underlying maladaptive coping strategies and symptoms of dysregulation. Traumatic experiences can dysregulate the vagus nerve and disrupt the balance between the ventral and dorsal vagal pathways, leading to difficulties in social engagement, emotional regulation, and self-soothing. Individuals who have experienced trauma may exhibit hyperactivation of the sympathetic nervous system and dorsal vagus, resulting in symptoms of anxiety, hypervigilance, and dissociation.

Furthermore, Polyvagal Theory emphasizes the importance of interventions that target the vagus nerve and promote regulation of the autonomic nervous system. Techniques such as deep breathing, mindfulness practices, and sensory modulation aim to activate the ventral vagus and promote feelings of safety and relaxation. By restoring balance to the autonomic nervous system, individuals can enhance their capacity for self-regulation and resilience in the face of stress and trauma. Moreover, understanding the role of the vagus nerve in trauma response can inform trauma-informed care approaches, empowering individuals to reclaim agency over their physiological and emotional well-being.

In summary, Stephen Porges' Polyvagal Theory offers a comprehensive framework for understanding the body's response to trauma and stress. By elucidating the role of the vagus nerve in regulating emotional and physiological states, this Theory provides valuable insights into the mechanisms underlying trauma-related symptoms and maladaptive coping strategies. Through interventions that promote regulation of the autonomic nervous system, individuals can cultivate greater resilience and well-being, fostering healing and recovery from traumatic experiences.

Trauma and The Brain

Trauma exerts a profound influence on the brain, reshaping its structure and function in ways that can have lasting implications for cognitive and emotional processing. Several key brain regions are particularly vulnerable to the effects of trauma, including the amygdala, hippocampus, and prefrontal cortex. The amygdala, situated deep within the brain's temporal lobes, plays a central role in processing emotions, particularly fear and threat detection. In response to traumatic experiences, the amygdala may become hyperactive, leading to exaggerated emotional responses, hypervigilance, and increased reactivity to potential threats. This heightened amygdala activity can contribute to symptoms of anxiety, hyperarousal, and emotional dysregulation commonly observed in individuals with a history of trauma.

Furthermore, trauma can profoundly impact the hippocampus, a key brain structure involved in memory formation and retrieval. The hippocampus plays a crucial role in encoding and consolidating memories, particularly those related to context and spatial navigation. However, exposure to traumatic events can impair hippocampal function, leading to deficits in memory consolidation and retrieval. Individuals with trauma-related disorders such as post-traumatic stress disorder (PTSD) may experience intrusive memories, flashbacks, or dissociative amnesia, reflecting disruptions in hippocampal-mediated memory processes. Moreover, alterations in hippocampal structure and function have been implicated in difficulties with spatial orientation, cognitive flexibility, and adaptive responding observed in trauma survivors.

Additionally, trauma can impact the prefrontal cortex, a region of the brain responsible for higher-order cognitive functions such as decision-making, impulse control, and emotion regulation. The prefrontal cortex acts as a regulatory hub, modulating the activity of subcortical structures such as the amygdala and hippocampus to facilitate adaptive responses to stress and threat. However, trauma-related alterations in prefrontal cortex function can impair executive functioning, inhibit impulse control, and compromise emotion regulation strategies. Individuals with a history of trauma may exhibit difficulties in inhibiting inappropriate responses, shifting attentional focus, and effectively modulating emotional arousal, leading to impairments in social functioning and adaptive coping.

Moreover, chronic exposure to trauma and stress can lead to structural and functional changes in the brain's neurocircuitry, including alterations in synaptic connectivity, neurochemical imbalances, and neuroinflammatory processes. These neurobiological changes can further exacerbate cognitive and emotional impairments associated with trauma, perpetuating a cycle of dysfunction and distress. However, emerging research suggests that the brain remains plastic throughout the lifespan, with the capacity for adaptive reorganization and recovery in response to therapeutic interventions and environmental enrichment. By understanding the neurobiological underpinnings of trauma-related brain alterations, clinicians and researchers can develop more targeted interventions aimed at promoting neuroplasticity, resilience, and recovery in trauma survivors.

Neuroplasticity and Healing

Neuroplasticity, the brain's remarkable ability to reorganize and adapt in response to experiences and environmental influences, offers profound implications for healing and recovery from trauma. Research has demonstrated that the nervous system retains a remarkable capacity for change throughout the lifespan, with the potential to rewire neural circuits, establish new connections, and generate neurons in response to therapeutic interventions and experiences. This inherent plasticity underlies the effectiveness of various therapeutic modalities in promoting healing and resilience in trauma survivors.

Therapy, particularly trauma-focused interventions such as cognitive-behavioral therapy (CBT), eye movement desensitization and reprocessing (EMDR), and prolonged exposure therapy, can facilitate neuroplasticity by providing individuals with opportunities to reprocess traumatic memories, challenge maladaptive beliefs, and develop adaptive coping strategies. Through the therapeutic relationship and guided interventions, individuals can harness the brain's plasticity to cultivate greater self-awareness, emotional regulation, and resilience in the face of adversity.

Mindfulness practices, such as meditation, yoga, and body scan exercises, offer another avenue for promoting neuroplasticity and healing from trauma. Mindfulness techniques encourage individuals to cultivate present-moment awareness, observe thoughts and sensations without judgment, and cultivate self-compassion. These practices have been shown to modulate neural activity in regions associated with attention, emotion regulation, and stress response, promoting greater neural integration and coherence. By engaging in regular mindfulness practice, individuals can strengthen neural networks involved in self-regulation and emotional well-being, fostering greater resilience and adaptive responses in the face of stress and trauma.

Somatic experiencing techniques, developed by Dr. Peter A. Levine, offer a body-centered approach to healing trauma that harnesses the innate wisdom of the nervous system. By focusing on bodily sensations, movement, and breath, somatic experiencing aims to discharge stored energy and release tension held within the body in response to trauma. Through gentle yet profound interventions, such as pendulation, titration, and tracking bodily sensations, individuals can renegotiate their relationship with trauma-related sensations, emotions, and memories, promoting greater integration and coherence within the nervous system.

Furthermore, environmental factors such as social support, physical activity, and environmental enrichment play a crucial role in promoting neuroplasticity and facilitating healing from trauma. Engaging in supportive relationships, participating in meaningful activities, and creating safe and nurturing environments can provide the scaffolding needed for neural repair and regeneration. By fostering environments rich in positive experiences and opportunities for growth, individuals can capitalize on the brain's inherent plasticity to cultivate resilience, restore balance, and embark on a journey toward healing and wholeness.

Chapter Five
The Minds of Children and Developmental Trauma

Trauma in Early Life and Its Long-Term Effects

Introduction to Developmental Trauma

Introduction to developmental trauma involves understanding the profound impact that adverse experiences during childhood can have on a child's psychological and emotional development. Developmental trauma refers to the chronic, repeated exposure to adverse events such as abuse, neglect, or household dysfunction during critical periods of a child's development. Unlike acute trauma, which typically involves a single traumatic event with a clear beginning and end, developmental trauma occurs over an extended period and often within the context of relationships that are meant to provide safety and security.

The distinction between developmental trauma and acute trauma lies in their duration, timing, and relational context. Acute trauma is often characterized by a sudden, overwhelming event, such as a car accident or a natural disaster, that triggers intense fear, helplessness, or horror. In contrast, developmental trauma unfolds gradually over time as children are repeatedly exposed to stressful or harmful experiences within their caregiving environment. These experiences may include physical or sexual abuse, emotional neglect, domestic violence, substance abuse, or mental illness within the family.

Developmental trauma disrupts the normal process of childhood development, particularly in areas related to attachment, emotional regulation, and cognitive functioning. Because the brain is still developing during childhood and adolescence, exposure to chronic stress and trauma can have lasting effects on neural pathways and brain structures. This can result in difficulties with emotional regulation, impulse control, attention, and decision-making, as well as an increased vulnerability to mental health disorders such as anxiety, depression, and post-traumatic stress disorder (PTSD).

Furthermore, developmental trauma can profoundly influence the formation of secure attachments and interpersonal relationships. Children who experience trauma early in life may struggle to trust others, have difficulty forming healthy relationships, and exhibit insecure attachment styles characterized by avoidance, ambivalence, or disorganization. These attachment difficulties can persist into adulthood, impacting the individual's ability to establish and maintain fulfilling relationships and contribute to feelings of loneliness, isolation, and disconnection.

In summary, understanding developmental trauma requires recognizing the cumulative impact of adverse experiences on a child's development and functioning. It involves acknowledging the complex interplay between early experiences, brain development, attachment relationships, and psychological well-being. By recognizing the unique challenges faced by individuals who have experienced developmental trauma, we can better tailor interventions and support systems to promote healing, resilience, and recovery.

Impact of Early Trauma

The impact of early trauma on children can be profound and far-reaching, encompassing a range of adverse experiences that can shape their development and well-being. These experiences include abuse, neglect, and witnessing violence, among others, each with its own set of consequences that can persist into adulthood. Abuse, whether physical, sexual, or emotional, inflicts direct harm on the child, often leaving lasting physical and psychological scars. Physical abuse can lead to injuries, chronic pain, and impaired physical health, while sexual abuse can result in trauma-related disorders such as PTSD, depression, anxiety, and difficulties with intimacy and trust.

Neglect, another form of early trauma, occurs when a child's basic needs for food, shelter, supervision, and affection are consistently unmet. Chronic neglect can undermine a child's sense of safety and security, leading to developmental delays, poor academic performance, and challenges in forming healthy relationships. Children who experience neglect may struggle with self-regulation, impulse control, and emotional expression, as well as feelings of worthlessness, shame, and abandonment.

Witnessing violence, whether between caregivers or in the community, can also have profound effects on children's development and well-being. Exposure to domestic violence, for example, can evoke feelings of fear, helplessness, and confusion, as well as internalizing and externalizing behaviors such as aggression, withdrawal, and difficulty concentrating. Witnessing violence can also increase the risk of experiencing violence oneself or developing mental health problems later in life.

The long-term consequences of early trauma are wide-ranging and can affect various aspects of a child's functioning, including physical health, mental health, social relationships, and academic achievement. Children who experience early trauma are at increased risk for a range of mental health disorders, including depression, anxiety, PTSD, substance abuse, and eating disorders. They may also struggle with academic performance, attendance, and behavior problems in school, leading to lower educational attainment and reduced opportunities for success in adulthood.

In conclusion, the impact of early trauma on children can be devastating, affecting every aspect of their lives and leaving lasting scars that persist into adulthood. It is crucial for caregivers, educators, and mental health professionals to recognize the signs of early trauma and provide appropriate support and intervention to help mitigate its effects and promote healing and resilience. By addressing early trauma with compassion, empathy, and evidence-based interventions, we can help children overcome adversity and reach their full potential.

Brain Development

Early trauma can profoundly impact brain development, particularly during critical periods of growth and maturation. The brain undergoes significant changes during childhood and adolescence, with rapid development occurring in regions responsible for emotional regulation, stress response, and attachment. Exposure to trauma during these formative years can disrupt the normal trajectory of brain development, leading to long-lasting alterations in neural circuits and functioning.

One key area affected by early trauma is the amygdala, a structure in the brain responsible for processing emotions and threat detection. Chronic stress and trauma can lead to hyperactivity and hypersensitivity in the amygdala, resulting in heightened emotional reactivity and difficulties with regulating emotions. This dysregulation can manifest as intense fear, anxiety, and impulsivity, making it challenging for children to cope with stressors and navigate social interactions.

Another area of the brain affected by early trauma is the prefrontal cortex, which plays a crucial role in executive functions such as impulse control, decision-making, and planning. Trauma can impair the development of the prefrontal cortex, leading to deficits in self-regulation and problem-solving skills. Children who have experienced trauma may struggle with impulsivity, poor judgment, and difficulty inhibiting inappropriate behaviors, which can impact their academic performance, social relationships, and overall functioning.

Furthermore, early trauma can disrupt the functioning of the hypothalamic-pituitary-adrenal (HPA) axis, the body's central stress response system. Prolonged exposure to stress and trauma can dysregulate the HPA axis, resulting in alterations in cortisol levels and heightened physiological arousal. This dysregulation can contribute to a heightened stress response, increased vulnerability to mental health disorders, and long-term health consequences such as cardiovascular disease and immune system dysfunction.

In addition to affecting emotional regulation and stress response, early trauma can also impact the development of attachment relationships. The attachment system, which is mediated by brain structures such as the hippocampus and the oxytocin system, is sensitive to early experiences of caregiving and relational trauma. Children who experience inconsistent, neglectful, or abusive caregiving may develop insecure attachment styles characterized by distrust, fear of abandonment, and difficulties forming close, intimate relationships.

In summary, early trauma can have profound and lasting effects on brain development, influencing emotional regulation, stress response, and attachment. By understanding the neurobiological mechanisms underlying the impact of trauma on the developing brain, we can better tailor interventions and support systems to promote healing, resilience, and recovery for children who have experienced trauma. Early identification and intervention are crucial in mitigating the long-term consequences of early trauma and fostering healthy development and well-being.

Psychological Effects

Developmental trauma can have profound psychological effects on children, impacting their emotional well-being, behavior, and cognitive functioning. One of the most common psychological effects of developmental trauma is anxiety. Children who have experienced trauma may exhibit excessive worry, fear, and hypervigilance, constantly anticipating threats and danger in their environment. This heightened state of arousal can interfere with daily functioning, impairing their ability to concentrate, sleep, and engage in social activities.

Depression is another common consequence of developmental trauma, characterized by persistent feelings of sadness, hopelessness, and despair. Children who have experienced trauma may struggle to experience pleasure or interest in activities they once enjoyed, withdrawing from social interactions and experiencing disruptions in their sleep and appetite. Depression can significantly impact a child's quality of life and academic performance, leading to difficulties in functioning at home, school, and in other areas of life.

Dissociation is a coping mechanism often observed in children who have experienced developmental trauma, allowing them to disconnect from overwhelming or distressing thoughts, feelings, and memories. Dissociation can manifest as a sense of numbness, detachment, or feeling disconnected from oneself or one's surroundings. Children may engage in daydreaming, spacing out, or experiencing gaps in memory as a way to cope with traumatic experiences and overwhelming emotions.

Difficulties with trust and relationships are common among children who have experienced developmental trauma stemming from disruptions in attachment relationships and experiences of betrayal, abandonment, or neglect. These children may struggle to trust others, fearing rejection or harm, and may exhibit defensive behaviors such as avoidance, aggression, or clinginess. Difficulty forming and maintaining healthy relationships can contribute to feelings of loneliness, isolation, and low self-esteem, further exacerbating the psychological impact of trauma.

Cognitive effects of developmental trauma can include difficulties with attention, memory, and executive functioning. Children who have experienced trauma may have trouble concentrating, following instructions, and completing tasks, leading to academic difficulties and challenges in school. Memory problems, such as difficulty recalling information or events, may also arise due to disruptions in brain functioning associated with trauma. These cognitive impairments can further hinder a child's ability to succeed academically and function effectively in daily life, perpetuating the cycle of stress and adversity.

In summary, developmental trauma can have far-reaching psychological effects on children, impacting their emotional well-being, behavior, and cognitive functioning. Understanding these effects is crucial for identifying and addressing the needs of children who have experienced trauma, as well as developing effective interventions and support systems to promote healing and resilience. By providing children with the necessary resources, support, and therapeutic interventions, we can help them overcome the psychological effects of trauma and thrive in spite of adversity.

Interpersonal Effects

Early trauma can profoundly affect children's interpersonal relationships, influencing how they interact with caregivers, peers, and authority figures and ultimately shaping their social functioning. One significant impact of early trauma is disruptions in attachment relationships with caregivers. Children who have experienced trauma may struggle to trust and form secure attachments with caregivers due to feelings of fear, betrayal, or abandonment. As a result, they may exhibit clingy, avoidant, or ambivalent behaviors in their interactions with caregivers, seeking comfort and reassurance one moment and pushing them away the next. These attachment difficulties can undermine the development of a secure base for exploration and emotional support, leading to challenges in regulating emotions and navigating relationships throughout childhood and beyond.

In addition to affecting relationships with caregivers, early trauma can also impact children's interactions with peers. Children who have experienced trauma may exhibit social withdrawal, aggression, or difficulties with peer interaction stemming from feelings of fear, mistrust, or low self-esteem. They may struggle to initiate and maintain friendships, interpret social cues accurately, or engage in cooperative play, leading to feelings of isolation, loneliness, and social rejection. These interpersonal difficulties can further exacerbate the psychological effects of trauma, reinforcing feelings of worthlessness, shame, and inadequacy.

Furthermore, early trauma can influence children's relationships with authority figures, such as teachers, coaches, and other adults in positions of power. Children who have experienced trauma may have difficulty trusting authority figures, perceiving them as threatening or unsafe, particularly if they have experienced abuse or neglect from adults in the past. This mistrust can lead to challenges in following rules and instructions, respecting boundaries, and seeking help when needed, undermining their academic performance, behavior, and overall well-being.

The implications of early trauma for social functioning extend beyond childhood, impacting various aspects of adult life, including intimate relationships, work, and community involvement. Adults who have experienced early trauma may struggle with intimacy, communication, and trust in romantic relationships, perpetuating patterns of insecure attachment and relationship dysfunction. They may also experience difficulties in the workplace, such as challenges in forming positive relationships with colleagues, managing stress and conflict, and asserting themselves effectively. Moreover, early trauma can affect community engagement and social support networks, as individuals may struggle to trust others, seek help when needed, or participate in social activities due to feelings of fear, shame, or unworthiness.

In summary, early trauma can have profound interpersonal effects on children, influencing their relationships with caregivers, peers, and authority figures and shaping their social functioning throughout life. Understanding these effects is essential for identifying and addressing the needs of children who have experienced trauma, as well as developing interventions and support systems to promote healing, resilience, and healthy social development. By providing children with safe, supportive relationships and opportunities for positive social interactions, we can help mitigate the impact of early trauma and foster positive outcomes in their interpersonal relationships and overall well-being.

Attachment Theory and Trauma

Overview of Attachment Theory

Attachment theory, developed by psychologist John Bowlby in the mid-20th century, offers valuable insights into the nature of human relationships, particularly those formed between caregivers and children. At its core, attachment theory posits that infants are biologically predisposed to seek proximity to their primary caregivers, typically their parents, in times of distress or threat. This innate drive for proximity serves an evolutionary purpose, promoting survival and protection by ensuring that infants receive the care and support they need for optimal development. The quality of the attachment bond formed between a child and caregiver during infancy lays the foundation for the child's social, emotional, and cognitive development throughout life.

Central to attachment theory is the concept of the "attachment behavioral system," which encompasses a set of innate behaviors and emotional responses designed to maintain closeness and security with caregivers. These behaviors include seeking comfort and reassurance from caregivers when distressed, as well as exploring the environment and engaging in social interactions when feeling safe and secure. Attachment theorists distinguish between different attachment styles that emerge based on the quality of the child's interactions with caregivers. The four primary attachment styles identified by psychologist Mary Ainsworth are secure attachment, insecure-avoidant attachment, insecure-anxious/ambivalent attachment, and disorganized attachment, each characterized by distinct patterns of behavior and emotional regulation.

The relevance of attachment theory to child development lies in its recognition of the critical role that early relationships play in shaping the child's social and emotional development. Secure attachment, characterized by trust, comfort, and a sense of safety in the caregiver's presence, provides a secure base from which children can explore the world, develop self-confidence, and regulate their emotions effectively. In contrast, insecure attachment styles, resulting from inconsistent, neglectful, or abusive caregiving, can lead to difficulties in emotional regulation, self-esteem, and forming healthy relationships. These early attachment patterns have far-reaching implications for the child's later social and emotional functioning, influencing their ability to establish and maintain relationships, cope with stress, and navigate interpersonal challenges.

Attachment theory also highlights the importance of sensitive and responsive caregiving in promoting secure attachment relationships. Caregivers who are attuned to their child's needs, provide consistent support and affection, and respond promptly to distress signals contribute to the development of secure attachment bonds. Conversely, caregivers who are insensitive, neglectful, or unresponsive to their child's needs may undermine the formation of secure attachments, leading to insecurity, mistrust, and emotional dysregulation in the child. Understanding the principles of attachment theory can inform parenting practices, interventions, and support systems aimed at promoting healthy attachment relationships and fostering positive outcomes for children's social and emotional development.

In summary, attachment theory provides a framework for understanding the dynamics of parent-child relationships and their impact on child development. By recognizing the importance of secure attachment bonds in promoting emotional security, resilience, and social competence, we can support caregivers in providing nurturing, responsive care that meets children's relational and emotional needs. Attachment theory underscores the fundamental role of early relationships in shaping the child's sense of self, their capacity for intimacy and trust, and their ability to navigate the complexities of social interactions throughout life.

Attachment Styles

Attachment styles, as defined by attachment theory, encompass patterns of behavior and emotional responses that individuals develop in relation to their primary caregivers during infancy and childhood. The four primary attachment styles identified by psychologist Mary Ainsworth are secure attachment, insecure-avoidant attachment, insecure-anxious/ambivalent attachment, and disorganized attachment. Secure attachment is characterized by a strong bond between the child and caregiver, marked by trust, comfort, and a sense of security in the caregiver's presence. Children with secure attachment styles feel confident exploring their environment, seek comfort from caregivers when distressed, and display resilience in the face of challenges.

In contrast, insecure-avoidant attachment is characterized by a lack of trust and emotional closeness between the child and caregiver. Children with this attachment style may avoid seeking comfort or reassurance from caregivers, preferring to self-soothe or engage in solitary activities. This avoidance of attachment figures may stem from experiences of caregivers who are consistently unavailable, unresponsive, or rejecting, leading the child to suppress their attachment needs and rely on themselves for emotional support.

Insecure-anxious/ambivalent attachment is marked by ambivalence and inconsistency in the child's relationship with the caregiver. Children with this attachment style may oscillate between seeking proximity to the caregiver and resisting comfort or reassurance when offered. They may display clingy, needy behavior, alternating between intense expressions of distress and anger and difficulty in settling even when comforted. This attachment style often develops in response to caregivers who are inconsistently available, responsive, or reliable, leading the child to become anxious about whether their needs will be met.

Disorganized attachment is characterized by a lack of organized attachment strategies, resulting in contradictory or disoriented behavior in the child's interactions with caregivers. Children with disorganized attachment may exhibit a confusing mix of approach and avoidance behaviors, showing signs of fear, confusion, or disorientation in the presence of their caregivers. Disorganized attachment often arises in the context of caregivers who are abusive, neglectful, or frightening, leading the child to experience intense internal conflict and uncertainty about their safety and the reliability of attachment figures.

Early trauma can significantly influence the development of attachment styles, as experiences of abuse, neglect, or inconsistent caregiving can disrupt the formation of secure attachment bonds. Children who experience trauma may develop insecure attachment styles, such as avoidant, anxious/ambivalent, or disorganized attachment, as a coping mechanism to navigate unpredictable or threatening caregiving environments. Trauma can undermine the child's ability to trust caregivers, regulate emotions, and develop a coherent sense of self within the attachment relationship, leading to challenges in forming healthy relationships and navigating social interactions throughout life. Understanding the impact of early trauma on attachment styles is crucial for providing appropriate interventions and support to help children heal from past experiences and develop secure, nurturing relationships that promote resilience and well-being.

Disrupted Attachment

Disrupted attachment, stemming from developmental trauma, can have profound and enduring effects on individuals' emotional and social development. Secure attachment, characterized by a strong bond between child and caregiver, provides a foundation for emotional security, trust, and resilience. However, developmental trauma, such as abuse, neglect, or inconsistent caregiving, can disrupt the formation of secure attachments, leading to attachment-related difficulties that persist into adulthood. When caregivers are unable to provide consistent, responsive care, children may develop insecure attachment styles, such as avoidant, anxious/ambivalent, or disorganized attachment, as adaptive responses to the unpredictable or threatening caregiving environment.

Children who experience disrupted attachment may exhibit a range of attachment-related difficulties, including challenges in regulating emotions, forming and maintaining relationships, and navigating social interactions. They may struggle to trust others, fear rejection or abandonment, and have difficulty expressing their needs and emotions openly. These difficulties can manifest in behaviors such as clinginess, withdrawal, aggression, or emotional dysregulation as children attempt to cope with the uncertainty and instability of their attachment relationships.

Moreover, disrupted attachment can have long-term consequences for individuals' mental health and well-being. Adults who experience disrupted attachment in childhood may continue to struggle with trust, intimacy, and emotional regulation in their relationships. They may have difficulty establishing boundaries, asserting their needs, and forming close, supportive connections with others. These attachment-related difficulties can contribute to feelings of loneliness, isolation, and low self-esteem as individuals grapple with the lingering effects of early trauma on their interpersonal relationships and sense of self.

In addition to impacting individuals' social and emotional functioning, disrupted attachment can also influence other areas of life, including academic and occupational success. Children who experience disrupted attachment may have difficulty focusing, regulating their behavior, and forming positive relationships with teachers and peers in school. These challenges can lead to academic underachievement, school dropout, and difficulties in the workplace later in life. Moreover, disrupted attachment may contribute to a cycle of intergenerational trauma, as individuals who experienced disrupted attachment in childhood may struggle to provide secure, nurturing care to their own children, perpetuating patterns of insecure attachment across generations.

In summary, disrupted attachment resulting from developmental trauma can have profound and pervasive effects on individuals' emotional, social, and psychological well-being. Understanding the impact of disrupted attachment is essential for identifying and addressing the needs of individuals who have experienced trauma, as well as developing interventions and support systems to promote healing, resilience, and healthy attachment relationships. By providing individuals with safe, supportive environments and opportunities for positive social interactions, we can help mitigate the impact of disrupted attachment and foster positive outcomes for their social and emotional development.

Impact on Identity Formation

Disrupted attachment resulting from developmental trauma can profoundly influence children's sense of self and identity formation. Secure attachment provides a secure base from which children can explore their environment and develop a coherent sense of self. However, when attachment relationships are disrupted due to experiences of abuse, neglect, or inconsistent caregiving, children may struggle to develop a stable sense of identity. Without the emotional security and validation provided by secure attachments, children may experience confusion, self-doubt, and low self-esteem, leading to difficulties in understanding their own needs, desires, and values.

Furthermore, disrupted attachment can impact children's ability to regulate emotions effectively. Secure attachment relationships serve as a source of comfort and support, helping children regulate their emotions and cope with stressors. However, when attachment relationships are characterized by inconsistency, unpredictability, or emotional neglect, children may develop maladaptive coping strategies, such as avoidance, dissociation, or emotional dysregulation. These difficulties in emotion regulation can manifest in symptoms such as anxiety, depression, impulsivity, and mood swings, undermining children's overall well-being and functioning.

Moreover, disrupted attachment can affect children's ability to form and maintain relationships with others. Secure attachment relationships provide a blueprint for healthy interpersonal connections, fostering trust, empathy, and reciprocity. However, when attachment relationships are disrupted, children may struggle to trust others, fear rejection or abandonment, and have difficulty forming close, intimate relationships. They may exhibit clingy, dependent behavior or withdraw from social interactions altogether as they struggle to navigate the complexities of interpersonal relationships without a secure foundation of attachment.

Additionally, disrupted attachment can impact children's sense of agency and autonomy. Secure attachment relationships promote a sense of efficacy and mastery, empowering children to explore their environment, assert their needs, and make choices that align with their values and preferences. However, when attachment relationships are characterized by power imbalances, coercion, or neglect, children may feel powerless, helpless, or overwhelmed by external demands. This sense of powerlessness can contribute to feelings of inadequacy, dependency, and difficulty asserting boundaries in relationships, perpetuating a cycle of vulnerability and insecurity.

In summary, disrupted attachment resulting from developmental trauma can have profound and enduring effects on children's identity formation, emotional regulation, and interpersonal relationships. Understanding the impact of disrupted attachment is crucial for providing appropriate interventions and support to help children heal from past experiences and develop secure, nurturing relationships that promote resilience and well-being. By addressing the underlying attachment difficulties and providing children with opportunities for positive social interactions and emotional support, we can help mitigate the impact of disrupted attachment and foster healthy identity development and relationship functioning.

Approaches to Treating Developmental Trauma

Therapeutic Approaches

Various therapeutic approaches have been developed to address the complex effects of developmental trauma on children's emotional and psychological well-being. Trauma-focused cognitive-behavioral therapy (TF-CBT) is one such approach that aims to help children process traumatic experiences and develop coping skills to manage distressing thoughts and emotions. TF-CBT utilizes a combination of cognitive-behavioral techniques, such as cognitive restructuring and exposure therapy, to challenge negative beliefs and reduce symptoms of anxiety, depression, and PTSD commonly associated with trauma. Through structured sessions with a trained therapist, children learn to identify and challenge unhelpful thought patterns, develop relaxation techniques, and gradually confront and process traumatic memories in a safe and supportive environment.

Play therapy is another therapeutic modality commonly used in treating developmental trauma, particularly with younger children who may have difficulty expressing themselves verbally. Play therapy provides children with a safe, non-threatening space to explore their thoughts, feelings, and experiences through play and creative expression. By engaging in play activities such as drawing, storytelling, and role-playing, children can externalize their internal struggles, process traumatic experiences, and develop new coping skills. Play therapy sessions are guided by a trained therapist who uses observation, reflection, and empathic listening to support children in making sense of their experiences and building resilience.

Eye movement desensitization and reprocessing (EMDR) is a therapeutic approach that has been shown to be effective in treating trauma-related symptoms, including flashbacks, nightmares, and hypervigilance. EMDR involves a series of standardized protocols that incorporate elements of cognitive-behavioral therapy, mindfulness, and bilateral stimulation to help children process traumatic memories and reprocess negative beliefs associated with the trauma. During EMDR sessions, children focus on specific traumatic memories while engaging in bilateral stimulation, such as following the therapist's hand movements or listening to auditory tones. This bilateral stimulation is thought to facilitate the processing and integration of traumatic memories, leading to a reduction in symptoms and an increased sense of control and mastery over one's experiences.

Attachment-based interventions are another important therapeutic approach used in treating developmental trauma, focusing on repairing and strengthening attachment relationships between children and caregivers. These interventions aim to provide caregivers with the support, skills, and understanding needed to create a safe and nurturing environment for their children. Through techniques such as reflective listening, empathic responding, and attunement, caregivers learn to recognize and respond to their children's emotional needs in a sensitive and consistent manner. By promoting secure attachment relationships, attachment-based interventions help children develop a sense of trust, safety, and emotional security, which serves as a foundation for healthy emotional and social development.

In summary, various therapeutic modalities have been developed to address the complex effects of developmental trauma on children's emotional and psychological well-being. Trauma-focused cognitive-behavioral therapy (TF-CBT), play therapy, eye movement desensitization and reprocessing (EMDR), and attachment-based interventions are just a few examples of the approaches used to help children process traumatic experiences, develop coping skills, and build resilience. By providing children with safe, supportive environments and evidence-based interventions, therapists can help mitigate the impact of developmental trauma and promote healing, growth, and recovery.

Importance of A Trauma-Informed Approach

The importance of a trauma-informed approach in working with children who have experienced developmental trauma cannot be overstated. Trauma-informed care emphasizes the recognition of the widespread impact of trauma on individuals' lives and the importance of understanding the unique needs and experiences of those who have been affected by trauma. For practitioners working with children, it is essential to recognize that trauma can profoundly affect every aspect of a child's development, including their emotional regulation, cognitive functioning, and interpersonal relationships. By approaching treatment from a trauma-informed perspective, practitioners can provide children with the support, validation, and empowerment they need to heal from past experiences and thrive in the present.

A trauma-informed approach also emphasizes the importance of creating safe, supportive environments that promote healing and recovery. Children who have experienced trauma may feel overwhelmed, anxious, or hypervigilant in certain settings, particularly those that remind them of past traumatic experiences. Practitioners must be attuned to these sensitivities and take steps to ensure that children feel safe, respected, and validated throughout the therapeutic process. This may involve creating predictable routines, providing clear communication, and offering opportunities for choice and autonomy, all of which can help children feel empowered and in control of their own healing journey.

Furthermore, a trauma-informed approach recognizes the interconnectedness of trauma and other social and environmental factors that influence children's well-being. Children who have experienced trauma may also face additional challenges, such as poverty, discrimination, or family instability, which can compound the impact of trauma on their lives. Practitioners must be mindful of these intersecting factors and work collaboratively with families, communities, and other service providers to address the multiple layers of trauma and adversity that children may be facing. By taking a holistic approach to treatment, practitioners can better support children in overcoming barriers to healing and achieving positive outcomes.

Moreover, a trauma-informed approach emphasizes the importance of building trusting, collaborative relationships with children and their families. Trust is foundational to the therapeutic process, particularly for children who may have experienced betrayal or abuse in their past relationships. Practitioners must demonstrate empathy, respect, and cultural sensitivity in their interactions with children and families, fostering a sense of safety and connection that allows for healing to occur. By actively involving children and families in treatment planning and decision-making, practitioners can empower them to take an active role in their own recovery and build resilience in the face of adversity.

In summary, a trauma-informed approach is essential for practitioners working with children who have experienced developmental trauma. By understanding the impact of trauma on children's development, creating safe and supportive environments, addressing intersecting social and environmental factors, and building trusting collaborative relationships, practitioners can provide children with the compassionate, effective care they need to heal from past experiences and thrive in the future.

Healing Relationships

Healing relationships, particularly those with caregivers and therapists, play a pivotal role in helping children recover from developmental trauma. Caregivers, including parents, foster parents, or other primary caregivers, serve as the first line of defense in providing safety, stability, and nurturing support to children who have experienced trauma. Consistent, responsive caregiving can help children develop a sense of trust, security, and emotional regulation, laying the foundation for healing and resilience. Caregivers who provide unconditional love, validation, and validation create a safe haven for children to express their emotions, process their experiences, and develop healthy coping mechanisms.

Therapists also play a crucial role in supporting children's recovery from developmental trauma. Therapeutic relationships built on trust, empathy, and unconditional positive regard provide children with a safe space to explore their thoughts, feelings, and experiences, free from judgment or criticism. Therapists use evidence-based interventions, such as trauma-focused cognitive-behavioral therapy (TF-CBT), play therapy, or eye movement desensitization and reprocessing (EMDR), to help children process traumatic memories, develop coping skills, and build resilience. Through therapeutic interventions, children learn to challenge negative beliefs, regulate their emotions, and develop adaptive strategies for managing stress and coping with adversity.

Moreover, supportive relationships with caregivers and therapists provide children with a sense of validation and empowerment, helping them reclaim a sense of agency and control over their own lives. Caregivers and therapists validate children's experiences, emotions, and reactions, affirming their worth and dignity as individuals. By providing children with opportunities for choice, autonomy, and self-expression, caregivers and therapists empower children to take an active role in their own healing journey, fostering a sense of mastery and self-efficacy.

Consistency and stability are also critical components of healing relationships for children recovering from developmental trauma. Children who have experienced trauma may have a heightened need for predictability, routine, and structure in their lives to feel safe and secure. Caregivers and therapists who provide consistent, reliable support help children build a sense of trust and stability, reducing feelings of uncertainty and anxiety. Consistent relationships with caregivers and therapists also allow children to develop secure attachment bonds, providing a foundation for healthy emotional and social development.

In summary, healing relationships with caregivers and therapists play a vital role in helping children recover from developmental trauma. Through supportive, consistent relationships, children receive the love, validation, and empowerment they need to heal from past experiences and build resilience for the future. By providing children with safe, nurturing environments and evidence-based interventions, caregivers and therapists can help children reclaim their sense of self-worth, agency, and hope, paving the way for a brighter, more secure future.

Holistic Interventions

Holistic interventions are essential in addressing developmental trauma as they recognize that trauma is not just an individual psychological issue but is deeply intertwined with social, environmental, and cultural factors. These interventions acknowledge that children who have experienced trauma often face multiple challenges beyond their psychological symptoms, including poverty, discrimination, family instability, and community violence. By addressing the broader context in which trauma occurs, holistic interventions can better support children's healing and promote resilience in the face of adversity.

One key aspect of holistic interventions is addressing the social factors that contribute to and exacerbate developmental trauma. Children who have experienced trauma may face social isolation, bullying, or discrimination, which can further compound their feelings of fear, shame, and helplessness. Holistic interventions aim to create supportive, inclusive environments that promote a sense of belonging, connection, and community for children. This may involve implementing anti-bullying programs, promoting diversity and inclusion initiatives, and fostering positive peer relationships within schools and communities.

Furthermore, holistic interventions recognize the importance of addressing environmental factors that impact children's well-being.

Children who have experienced trauma may live in unsafe, unstable environments characterized by poverty, crime, or inadequate housing. Holistic interventions aim to address these environmental stressors by providing children and families with access to safe housing, nutritious food, healthcare, and other basic needs. By addressing these foundational needs, holistic interventions create a more stable, supportive environment for children to heal and thrive.

Cultural factors also play a significant role in shaping children's experiences of trauma and their responses to intervention. Cultural beliefs, values, and traditions influence how trauma is understood, expressed, and addressed within different communities. Holistic interventions recognize the importance of cultural sensitivity and responsiveness in working with children who have experienced trauma. This may involve incorporating culturally relevant practices, rituals, and healing traditions into therapeutic interventions, as well as partnering with community leaders and organizations to ensure that interventions are culturally appropriate and accessible to all children and families.

In summary, holistic interventions are essential in addressing developmental trauma as they recognize the interconnectedness of psychological, social, environmental, and cultural factors that contribute to children's experiences of trauma. By addressing the broader context in which trauma occurs, holistic interventions can better support children's healing, resilience, and well-being. By creating safe, supportive environments that promote belonging, addressing environmental stressors, and incorporating cultural sensitivity into interventions, holistic interventions help children and families navigate the complex challenges of trauma and build a brighter, more hopeful future.

Prevention and Early Intervention

Prevention and early intervention are critical components in mitigating the long-term effects of developmental trauma and promoting resilience in children. Early identification of trauma and timely intervention can significantly impact a child's trajectory by providing them with the necessary support and resources to heal from their experiences. By addressing trauma early in a child's life, practitioners can prevent the escalation of symptoms and reduce the risk of chronic mental health issues, such as anxiety, depression, and PTSD, that may persist into adulthood.

Early intervention is especially crucial because trauma experienced during childhood can have lasting effects on brain development, emotional regulation, and social functioning. The brain undergoes significant development during early childhood, and exposure to trauma during this critical period can disrupt the formation of neural circuits and pathways, leading to difficulties in emotional regulation and stress response. Early intervention can help mitigate these disruptions by providing children with tools and strategies to cope with their experiences and regulate their emotions effectively.

Furthermore, early identification and intervention can help address the underlying factors that contribute to and exacerbate developmental trauma, such as poverty, family instability, and community violence. By providing children and families with access to support services, such as counseling, parenting education, and social services, practitioners can address these risk factors and create a more supportive, nurturing environment for children to thrive. Early intervention can also help break the cycle of intergenerational trauma by providing parents and caregivers with the skills and resources they need to provide safe, stable caregiving to their children.

Prevention efforts are equally important in addressing developmental trauma and promoting resilience in children. By implementing programs and policies that address the root causes of trauma, such as poverty, discrimination, and inequality, communities can create more equitable and supportive environments for children and families. Prevention efforts may include early childhood education programs, mental health screenings in schools, and community-based initiatives that promote positive parenting practices and family support networks. By investing in prevention efforts, communities can reduce the prevalence of trauma and create a healthier, more resilient society for future generations.

In summary, prevention and early intervention are essential in addressing developmental trauma and promoting resilience in children. By identifying trauma early in a child's life and providing timely, evidence-based interventions, practitioners can mitigate the long-term effects of trauma and help children heal from their experiences. Moreover, prevention efforts aimed at addressing the root causes of trauma can create more supportive, nurturing environments for children to thrive, ultimately leading to healthier, more resilient communities for all.

Chapter Six
Dissociation and Fragmented Selves

The Phenomenon of Dissociation in Trauma Survivors

Definition of Dissociation

Dissociation is a psychological phenomenon characterized by a disruption or detachment from one's thoughts, feelings, memories, or identity. At its core, dissociation involves a disconnection between various aspects of consciousness, leading to a sense of detachment from oneself or the surrounding environment. This disconnection can manifest in various forms, ranging from mild experiences of spacing out or daydreaming to more severe disruptions in perception and identity. Dissociation often arises as a coping mechanism in response to overwhelming stress, trauma, or distressing experiences. Individuals may unconsciously dissociate as a way to distance themselves from distressing emotions or memories, allowing them to temporarily escape from reality or numb themselves to painful feelings.

Exploring dissociation as a coping mechanism reveals its adaptive function in helping individuals manage overwhelming emotions or traumatic events. By disconnecting from their immediate experience, individuals may create a mental space where they can retreat to a safer internal environment. This coping strategy serves as a form of psychological self-protection, allowing individuals to regulate their emotions and maintain a sense of control in the face of adversity. However, while dissociation may provide temporary relief from distress, it can also lead to a fragmented sense of self and impair functioning in daily life. Understanding the underlying motivations and triggers for dissociation is crucial in developing effective interventions to address its impact on individuals' well-being.

Dissociative experiences encompass a spectrum of phenomena, including depersonalization, derealization, and amnesia. Depersonalization involves a sense of detachment or estrangement from one's own body, thoughts, or sensations, often described as feeling like an outside observer of oneself. Derealization, on the other hand, involves a perception of the external world as unreal, dreamlike, or distorted, leading to feelings of detachment from one's surroundings. Both depersonalization and derealization can profoundly affect individuals' sense of reality and identity, contributing to feelings of unreality or disconnection from oneself and the world. Additionally, dissociative amnesia entails gaps or lapses in memory, where individuals may be unable to recall important personal information, significant events, or periods of time, often associated with traumatic experiences or high levels of stress.

Recognizing the diverse manifestations of dissociative experiences is essential in accurately assessing and addressing individuals' needs in clinical settings. Differentiating between various types of dissociation can inform treatment planning and intervention strategies tailored to each individual's unique experiences and symptoms. By acknowledging the multifaceted nature of dissociation and its underlying mechanisms, mental health professionals can provide compassionate and effective support to help individuals navigate and integrate their dissociative experiences into their broader sense of self and reality.

The Prevalence of Dissociation in Trauma Survivors

The prevalence of dissociation among trauma survivors underscores the profound impact of adverse experiences on psychological well-being. Research indicates that dissociative symptoms are remarkably common among individuals who have experienced trauma, with prevalence rates varying depending on the nature and severity of the traumatic event. Studies have consistently found elevated levels of dissociation in populations exposed to interpersonal violence, such as survivors of childhood abuse, sexual assault, and domestic violence. Furthermore, dissociation is frequently observed in individuals with post-traumatic stress disorder (PTSD), with research suggesting that dissociative symptoms often co-occur with other trauma-related psychiatric conditions.

Statistics and research findings provide valuable insights into the prevalence and correlates of dissociation in trauma survivors. Epidemiological studies have documented high rates of dissociative symptoms in clinical and non-clinical populations, highlighting the widespread nature of this phenomenon. For example, a meta-analysis examining the prevalence of dissociation in individuals exposed to trauma found that approximately 60-80% of trauma survivors report experiencing dissociative symptoms at some point in their lives. Moreover, longitudinal research has shown that dissociative symptoms are associated with increased severity of PTSD symptoms, functional impairment, and decreased quality of life, underscoring the significance of addressing dissociation in trauma-focused interventions.

Common experiences that may lead to dissociation encompass a wide range of traumatic events and stressors that overwhelm individuals' capacity to cope effectively. Childhood abuse, including physical, sexual, and emotional maltreatment, is recognized as a potent risk factor for the development of dissociative symptoms later in life. The chronic and pervasive nature of childhood trauma can disrupt the formation of secure attachment bonds and contribute to profound disruptions in identity and self-concept. Similarly, exposure to combat-related trauma, such as military combat or warzone experiences, can trigger dissociative responses as individuals struggle to reconcile the horrors of war with their pre-existing beliefs and values. Additionally, natural disasters, accidents, and other life-threatening events can evoke acute dissociative reactions as individuals confront the sudden and overwhelming loss of safety and security.

Understanding the complex interplay between traumatic experiences and dissociative responses is crucial in providing comprehensive and trauma-informed care to survivors. Clinicians working with trauma survivors must assess for dissociative symptoms and tailor interventions to address the unique needs and challenges associated with dissociation. By fostering a supportive and validating therapeutic environment, mental health professionals can help survivors navigate the process of healing and recovery, empowering them to reclaim agency and rebuild a sense of coherence and connection in their lives. Additionally, promoting resilience and coping skills can enhance individuals' capacity to regulate emotions and manage distressing symptoms, fostering adaptive functioning and well-being in the aftermath of trauma.

Understanding the Neurobiological Basis of Dissociation

Understanding the neurobiological basis of dissociation sheds light on the intricate interplay between brain functioning and psychological processes. Neuroimaging studies have identified several key brain regions implicated in dissociative experiences, providing valuable insights into the neural mechanisms underlying this phenomenon. One such region is the prefrontal cortex, particularly the dorsolateral prefrontal cortex (DLPFC), which plays a crucial role in executive functions such as attentional control, decision-making, and emotion regulation. Dysfunction in the DLPFC has been associated with impairments in cognitive control and emotion regulation, contributing to the manifestation of dissociative symptoms. Additionally, alterations in the default mode network (DMN), a network of brain regions involved in self-referential processing and introspection, have been implicated in dissociation. Disruptions in the connectivity and activity of the DMN may underlie distortions in self-awareness and identity experienced during dissociative states.

Trauma exerts profound effects on the brain's response to stress and threat, leading to dysregulation in neural circuits involved in emotional processing and stress modulation. The amygdala, a key brain structure involved in the processing of threat-related stimuli and the regulation of emotional responses, exhibits heightened activation in response to traumatic cues in individuals with PTSD and dissociative symptoms. This hyperresponsivity of the amygdala contributes to the heightened emotional reactivity and hypervigilance commonly observed in trauma survivors. Moreover, alterations in the functioning of the hippocampus, a brain region critical for memory encoding and retrieval, have been implicated in dissociative amnesia and memory disturbances following trauma. Chronic stress and trauma exposure have been shown to impair hippocampal function, leading to deficits in memory consolidation and retrieval processes.

Furthermore, dysregulation of the hypothalamic-pituitary-adrenal (HPA) axis, the body's primary stress response system, has been implicated in the pathophysiology of dissociative symptoms. Trauma survivors often exhibit alterations in cortisol levels and HPA axis functioning, reflecting dysregulation in stress hormone secretion and response patterns. Chronic stress and trauma can lead to HPA axis hyperactivity or hypoactivity, disrupting the body's ability to effectively regulate stress responses and maintain homeostasis. These neurobiological changes contribute to the development and maintenance of dissociative symptoms, as heightened arousal and dysregulated stress responses exacerbate emotional dysregulation and impair cognitive functioning.

In summary, the neurobiological basis of dissociation involves complex interactions between brain regions implicated in emotional regulation, self-awareness, and stress modulation. Dysregulation in neural circuits underlying these processes contributes to the manifestation of dissociative symptoms in trauma survivors. Understanding the neurobiological mechanisms of dissociation not only enhances our theoretical understanding of this phenomenon but also informs the development of targeted interventions aimed at addressing underlying neural dysfunctions and promoting recovery and resilience in individuals affected by trauma-related dissociative disorders.

Factors Influencing the Severity of Dissociative Symptoms

The severity of dissociative symptoms is influenced by a myriad of factors that encompass individual differences in resilience and vulnerability, as well as the nature and intensity of traumatic experiences. Resilience, defined as the ability to adapt and thrive in the face of adversity, plays a significant role in mitigating the impact of trauma and moderating the severity of dissociative symptoms. Individuals with higher levels of resilience may possess stronger coping mechanisms, social support networks, and adaptive strategies for managing stress, thereby exhibiting fewer and less severe dissociative symptoms following trauma exposure. Conversely, individuals with lower levels of resilience may be more susceptible to the deleterious effects of trauma, experiencing heightened distress and dissociation in response to adverse experiences.

Vulnerability factors, such as genetic predispositions, early life experiences, and psychosocial stressors, also contribute to the severity of dissociative symptoms. Genetic studies have identified heritable traits and polymorphisms associated with increased susceptibility to stress-related psychiatric disorders, including dissociative disorders. Early life adversity, such as childhood abuse, neglect, and insecure attachment, can shape neurodevelopmental pathways and increase vulnerability to dissociative symptoms later in life. Additionally, ongoing psychosocial stressors, such as poverty, discrimination, and social isolation, can exacerbate dissociative symptoms and impair resilience, perpetuating a cycle of vulnerability and maladaptive coping.

The relationship between trauma severity and dissociation is complex and multifaceted, with trauma severity serving as a significant predictor of dissociative symptomatology. Traumatic experiences characterized by extreme threats to physical integrity, loss of safety, or betrayal of trust are more likely to elicit dissociative responses as adaptive coping mechanisms. Moreover, the duration, frequency, and intensity of trauma exposure are positively associated with the severity of dissociative symptoms, with chronic and repeated trauma resulting in more pronounced dissociative disturbances. Complex trauma, involving multiple and intersecting forms of adversity, such as childhood maltreatment, interpersonal violence, and community violence, is particularly detrimental to psychological well-being and may contribute to the development of complex dissociative disorders, such as dissociative identity disorder (DID).

Furthermore, the developmental timing of trauma exposure plays a crucial role in shaping the severity and trajectory of dissociative symptoms. Early onset trauma, occurring during critical periods of neurodevelopment, can disrupt the formation of self-identity, attachment bonds, and emotion regulation capacities, leading to profound disturbances in consciousness and identity. Additionally, the presence of comorbid psychiatric conditions, such as post-traumatic stress disorder (PTSD), depression, and substance use disorders, can exacerbate dissociative symptoms and complicate clinical presentations. Understanding the interplay between trauma severity, individual differences in resilience and vulnerability, and developmental factors is essential for assessing and addressing the diverse needs of trauma survivors experiencing dissociative symptoms. By recognizing and addressing these underlying factors, mental health professionals can tailor interventions to promote resilience, enhance coping skills, and facilitate recovery and healing in individuals affected by trauma-related dissociative disorders.

Understanding Fragmented Self-Identity

Defining Fragmented Self-Identity

Defining fragmented self-identity involves understanding the intricate relationship between various aspects of an individual's sense of self that may become disjointed or disconnected due to internal or external influences. At its core, fragmented self-identity refers to a state in which different facets of one's identity, such as thoughts, emotions, memories, and beliefs, fail to integrate into a cohesive and unified whole. Instead, these components may exist in isolation or conflict with each other, leading to a sense of inconsistency, instability, or disconnection within the individual's sense of self. Fragmentation can manifest in different ways, ranging from mild experiences of self-doubt or confusion to more severe disruptions in identity, such as dissociative identity disorder (DID), where distinct personality states emerge and alternate control over the individual's behavior and consciousness.

Exploring the concept of identity fragmentation delves into the complex interplay of psychological, developmental, and environmental factors that contribute to the fragmentation of self-identity. Childhood experiences, particularly those involving attachment disruptions, abuse, neglect, or invalidation, can profoundly shape the formation of self-concept and identity. Adverse experiences during critical periods of development may hinder the integration of self-representation, resulting in the fragmentation of identity and the emergence of maladaptive coping strategies, such as dissociation, to manage overwhelming emotions or threats to the integrity of self. Additionally, societal and cultural influences, such as stigma, discrimination, and social marginalization, can exacerbate identity fragmentation by imposing external expectations and constraints on individuals' sense of self and identity expression.

Dissociation contributes to a fragmented sense of self by disrupting the continuity and coherence of conscious experience, leading to compartmentalization or segregation of aspects of identity. Individuals experiencing dissociation may feel detached from their thoughts, emotions, memories, or bodily sensations, resulting in a sense of estrangement or disconnection from themselves and their surroundings. Depersonalization and derealization experiences, characterized by feelings of unreality or detachment from oneself and the external world, can exacerbate identity fragmentation by creating a sense of disembodiment or dissociation from one's own lived experience. Furthermore, dissociative amnesia, involving lapses in memory or gaps in consciousness, can contribute to discontinuities in the narrative of one's life story, further fragmenting the sense of self and identity coherence.

Moreover, trauma-related dissociation often involves the formation of dissociative parts or self-states, each with its own unique set of memories, emotions, beliefs, and behaviors. These dissociated parts may emerge as adaptive responses to overwhelming or traumatic experiences, serving to compartmentalize and contain distressing thoughts or emotions that would otherwise overwhelm the individual's capacity to cope. However, while dissociation may provide temporary relief from distress, it can also lead to fragmentation and fragmentation of self-identity, resulting in a fragmented sense of self and impaired functioning in daily life. Understanding the complex interplay between dissociation and identity fragmentation is crucial in assessing and addressing the needs of individuals affected by trauma-related dissociative disorders, facilitating integration and coherence of self-identity, and promoting recovery and healing.

The Role of Attachment in Identity Formation

The role of attachment in identity formation is fundamental, shaping the way individuals perceive themselves and interact with the world. Attachment theory, pioneered by John Bowlby, posits that early experiences with caregivers lay the foundation for the development of internal working models of self and others, which influence subsequent social and emotional functioning. Secure attachment, characterized by responsive and attuned caregiving, fosters a sense of safety, trust, and worthiness in the child, providing a secure base from which to explore the world and form relationships. In contrast, insecure attachment, marked by inconsistent, neglectful, or abusive caregiving, can impede the development of a coherent and positive self-concept, leading to difficulties in regulating emotions, managing relationships, and navigating social interactions. These early attachment experiences shape individuals' beliefs about themselves, others, and the world, influencing their sense of identity, self-worth, and belonging.

The impact of early attachment experiences on self-concept is profound, laying the groundwork for how individuals perceive and relate to themselves throughout their lives. Securely attached individuals tend to have a positive and coherent self-concept characterized by feelings of competence, autonomy, and relational security. They are more likely to view themselves as lovable, capable, and deserving of care and support, fostering a sense of resilience and adaptability in the face of challenges. In contrast, insecurely attached individuals may struggle with self-doubt, worthlessness, and a pervasive sense of inadequacy stemming from internalized beliefs about their unlovability, unworthiness, or inability to meet others' needs. These negative self-schemas can undermine self-esteem, self-efficacy, and self-compassion, contributing to psychological distress and interpersonal difficulties.

Disruptions in attachment contribute to identity fragmentation by undermining the formation of a coherent and stable sense of self. Early experiences of neglect, abandonment, or abuse can erode the trust and security necessary for healthy identity development, leading to a fragmented self-concept marked by conflicting or unstable self-representations. Insecurely attached individuals may struggle with identity confusion, identity diffusion, or identity foreclosure as they grapple with unresolved questions about who they are, what they value, and where they belong. Moreover, disruptions in attachment can impair emotion regulation abilities, exacerbating dissociative symptoms and further fragmenting the sense of self. Individuals may resort to maladaptive coping strategies, such as dissociation, to cope with overwhelming emotions or relational stressors, leading to compartmentalization of identity and fragmented experiences of selfhood.

Furthermore, disruptions in attachment can perpetuate cycles of relational dysfunction and interpersonal difficulties, further exacerbating identity fragmentation. Insecurely attached individuals may struggle to establish and maintain healthy boundaries, assert their needs and preferences, or form trusting and intimate relationships.

Their relationships may be marked by dependency, mistrust, or emotional distance, reflecting unresolved attachment patterns and internalized beliefs about their own unworthiness or unlovability. These relational challenges can reinforce feelings of alienation, isolation, and disconnection, exacerbating identity fragmentation and perpetuating a cycle of relational distress. Understanding the impact of disruptions in attachment on identity formation and fragmentation is essential in providing compassionate and effective support to individuals struggling with unresolved attachment issues and promoting healing and integration of self-identity. Through supportive relationships, therapeutic interventions, and self-reflection, individuals can begin to reconcile their past experiences, cultivate self-awareness and acceptance, and foster a more coherent and authentic sense of self.

Cultural and Societal Influences on Self-Identity

Cultural and societal influences play a significant role in shaping self-identity, as they provide individuals with frameworks, values, and norms through which to understand themselves and their place in the world. Cultural identity encompasses the beliefs, customs, traditions, and practices shared by members of a particular cultural group, influencing individuals' sense of belonging, meaning, and purpose. Societal factors, such as gender roles, socioeconomic status, ethnicity, religion, and nationality, also contribute to the construction of self-identity, as they shape individuals' experiences, opportunities, and social roles within their communities. Cultural and societal influences provide individuals with a sense of belonging and affiliation, shaping their perceptions of self and others and influencing their behavior, values, and aspirations.

Cultural norms and expectations play a pivotal role in shaping identity by prescribing roles, behaviors, and attributes deemed appropriate or desirable within a particular cultural context. These norms provide individuals with guidelines for navigating social interactions, expressing themselves, and fulfilling societal roles and responsibilities. For example, cultural norms surrounding gender roles may dictate expectations for masculinity and femininity, influencing individuals' self-concept, expression of gender identity, and social roles. Similarly, cultural expectations regarding success, achievement, and status may shape individuals' aspirations, values, and self-esteem, influencing their pursuit of academic, professional, or personal goals. Moreover, cultural norms and expectations may intersect with other social identities, such as race, ethnicity, sexuality, and disability, shaping individuals' experiences of marginalization, privilege, and social belonging.

The stigma surrounding dissociative disorders can have profound effects on individuals' self-perception and mental health outcomes. Dissociative disorders, such as dissociative identity disorder (DID), are often misunderstood, stigmatized, and misrepresented in popular culture and media, perpetuating myths, stereotypes, and misconceptions about the nature and validity of these conditions. The stigma surrounding dissociative disorders can lead to feelings of shame, secrecy, and self-blame, as individuals may internalize negative beliefs and attitudes about their symptoms or diagnosis. Moreover, stigma can impede help-seeking behaviors, as individuals may fear judgment, rejection, or discrimination from others, leading to delays in accessing appropriate support and treatment. The experience of stigma can exacerbate feelings of isolation, alienation, and invalidation, further undermining individuals' sense of self-worth, identity coherence, and psychological well-being.

Furthermore, cultural and societal factors can influence the experience and expression of dissociative symptoms, shaping individuals' perceptions of their symptoms and their willingness to seek help. Cultural beliefs about mental health, illness, and treatment may impact individuals' attitudes towards dissociation, shaping their interpretation of symptoms as normal or pathological. Cultural differences in language, communication styles, and help-seeking behaviors may also affect individuals' ability to articulate their experiences of dissociation and access culturally sensitive and appropriate care. Additionally, societal attitudes towards trauma, abuse, and victimization may contribute to victim-blaming narratives and disbelief, further exacerbating feelings of shame, guilt, and self-doubt among individuals with dissociative disorders. Recognizing the cultural and societal influences on self-identity and the stigma surrounding dissociative disorders is essential in providing culturally competent and stigma-free support and resources to individuals affected by these conditions, fostering empowerment, validation, and recovery. Through education, advocacy, and destigmatization efforts, we can create more inclusive and supportive environments that honor the diversity of human experiences and promote mental health and well-being for all.

The Subjective Experience of Fragmented Self-Identity

The subjective experience of fragmented self-identity encompasses a complex array of thoughts, emotions, and perceptions that individuals with dissociative disorders navigate on a daily basis. For those with conditions like dissociative identity disorder (DID), the sense of self can feel disjointed, fragmented, and, at times, deeply fractured. Individuals may experience shifts in identity, memory lapses, and a sense of detachment from their own thoughts, feelings, and actions. These experiences can lead to confusion, distress, and a pervasive sense of not truly knowing oneself. The fragmented self-identity is often described as akin to living with multiple selves or identities, each with its own distinct traits, memories, and behaviors, which can cause significant disruptions in daily functioning and interpersonal relationships.

Personal narratives and firsthand accounts of individuals with dissociative identity disorder (DID) provide invaluable insights into the lived experience of fragmented self-identity. These narratives offer glimpses into the internal struggles, coping mechanisms, and resilience of individuals navigating the complexities of dissociation. Through their stories, individuals with DID shed light on the challenges of reconciling conflicting identities, managing memory gaps, and navigating interpersonal dynamics. They also highlight the profound impact of trauma and adversity on the formation and fragmentation of self-identity, as well as the resilience and strength inherent in their journeys toward healing and integration. Personal narratives serve to humanize the experience of dissociative disorders, dispelling myths and misconceptions and fostering empathy and understanding within broader society.

Challenges and struggles associated with fragmented self-identity are manifold and multifaceted, encompassing psychological, social, and existential dimensions. Individuals with dissociative disorders may grapple with feelings of disorientation, existential confusion, and a pervasive sense of emptiness or void within themselves. They may experience identity crises, wherein the boundaries between self and another blur, leading to feelings of existential dread and a loss of sense of agency or control. Moreover, the episodic nature of dissociative symptoms can disrupt the continuity of self-experience, leading to disruptions in daily functioning, work, and relationships. The struggle to maintain a coherent and integrated sense of self amidst the chaos of dissociation can be profoundly isolating and alienating, exacerbating feelings of loneliness, shame, and inadequacy.

Furthermore, individuals with fragmented self-identity often face stigma, disbelief, and invalidation from others, compounding their sense of isolation and marginalization. The invisibility of dissociative symptoms, coupled with societal misconceptions and biases, can lead to a lack of recognition and support from friends, family, and healthcare providers. This can further exacerbate feelings of shame, self-doubt, and internalized stigma, hindering individuals' ability to seek help and access appropriate treatment. Additionally, navigating the complexities of identity disclosure and managing the impact of dissociative symptoms on interpersonal relationships can pose significant challenges, as individuals may fear rejection, judgment, or abandonment if their experiences are not understood or accepted by others.

In conclusion, the subjective experience of fragmented self-identity is a deeply nuanced and often tumultuous journey marked by internal conflict, existential questioning, and external challenges. Personal narratives of individuals with dissociative identity disorder (DID) offer valuable insights into the complexities of living with dissociation and the resilience inherent in the process of healing and integration. However, the challenges and struggles associated with fragmented self-identity are profound and multifaceted, encompassing psychological, social, and existential dimensions. By fostering empathy, awareness, and understanding, we can create more inclusive and supportive environments that honor the diversity of human experiences and promote healing and integration for individuals affected by dissociative disorders.

Treatment Approaches for Dissociative Symptoms

Psychotherapy for Dissociation

Psychotherapy for dissociation is a multifaceted and nuanced approach aimed at addressing the complex interplay of psychological, emotional, and interpersonal factors contributing to dissociative symptoms. One of the primary goals of psychotherapy is to help individuals with dissociation gain insight into their experiences, develop coping strategies, and integrate fragmented aspects of their self-identity. Therapeutic modalities vary in their theoretical orientations, techniques, and treatment goals, but they all share a common focus on creating a safe and supportive therapeutic environment conducive to healing and recovery.

An overview of different therapeutic modalities reveals a diverse array of approaches tailored to the unique needs and preferences of individuals with dissociative disorders. Cognitive-behavioral therapy (CBT) focuses on identifying and challenging maladaptive thoughts, beliefs, and behaviors contributing to dissociation. Through cognitive restructuring, individuals learn to recognize and modify dysfunctional cognitive patterns, develop coping skills for managing distressing emotions, and cultivate a sense of agency and control over their experiences. Dialectical behavior therapy (DBT) integrates cognitive-behavioral techniques with mindfulness-based practices, emphasizing acceptance, validation, and emotional regulation. DBT helps individuals develop interpersonal effectiveness skills, distress tolerance techniques, and emotion regulation strategies to navigate challenging situations and reduce dissociative symptoms.

Eye Movement Desensitization and Reprocessing (EMDR) is a specialized form of therapy that targets traumatic memories and experiences underlying dissociative symptoms. EMDR combines elements of cognitive-behavioral therapy with bilateral stimulation techniques, such as eye movements or tactile sensations, to facilitate the processing and integration of traumatic memories. By accessing and reprocessing traumatic memories within a safe therapeutic context, individuals can reduce the emotional intensity and cognitive distortions associated with traumatic experiences, leading to symptom relief and improved self-awareness. EMDR also incorporates elements of resourcing and stabilization to enhance individuals' capacity to regulate emotions and manage dissociative symptoms during the therapeutic process.

The role of trauma-focused therapy in addressing dissociation is central to promoting healing and integration in individuals affected by dissociative disorders. Trauma-focused therapy aims to address the underlying trauma and attachment disruptions contributing to dissociative symptoms, fostering a sense of safety, empowerment, and trust within the therapeutic relationship. Through a collaborative and phased approach, therapists help individuals gradually process and integrate traumatic memories, develop coping skills for managing distress, and strengthen adaptive resources for resilience and recovery. Trauma-focused therapy also emphasizes psychoeducation, validation, and normalization of dissociative experiences, helping individuals understand the connection between trauma and dissociation and reducing feelings of shame, self-blame, and isolation.

Moreover, trauma-focused therapy incorporates elements of stabilization, grounding, and containment to provide individuals with a sense of safety and stability as they navigate the complexities of trauma processing. Therapists work collaboratively with clients to develop personalized safety plans, establish healthy coping mechanisms, and build supportive networks to mitigate the risk of destabilization or retraumatization during therapy. By addressing the root causes of dissociation and providing individuals with the tools and resources needed to navigate their experiences, trauma-focused therapy facilitates healing, integration, and empowerment, empowering individuals to reclaim agency and autonomy in their lives.

Pharmacological Interventions

Pharmacological interventions serve as an adjunctive treatment modality for individuals with dissociative disorders, aiming to alleviate symptoms and enhance overall functioning. While psychotherapy remains the cornerstone of treatment for dissociation, medications can play a valuable role in managing co-occurring symptoms, such as depression, anxiety, and sleep disturbances, which often accompany dissociative disorders. However, it's essential to approach medication management with caution and carefully consider the potential benefits and risks, as well as individual differences in treatment response and medication tolerance.

Antidepressants are among the most commonly prescribed medications for managing dissociative symptoms, particularly those associated with mood dysregulation, depression, and anxiety. Selective serotonin reuptake inhibitors (SSRIs) and serotonin-norepinephrine reuptake inhibitors (SNRIs) are frequently used due to their efficacy in addressing mood symptoms and their relatively favorable side effect profiles. SSRIs, such as fluoxetine (Prozac) and sertraline (Zoloft), help regulate serotonin levels in the brain, which can improve mood stability and reduce symptoms of depression and anxiety. SNRIs, such as venlafaxine (Effexor) and duloxetine (Cymbalta), target both serotonin and norepinephrine reuptake, offering additional benefits for individuals with comorbid anxiety and chronic pain conditions.

Antipsychotic medications may also be prescribed to manage dissociative symptoms, particularly those associated with psychosis, agitation, or severe dissociative experiences. Atypical antipsychotics, such as risperidone (Risperdal) and olanzapine (Zyprexa), are often used to address psychotic symptoms, such as hallucinations or delusions, which may occur in the context of dissociative disorders. These medications work by blocking dopamine receptors in the brain, helping to reduce the severity and frequency of psychotic symptoms and stabilizing mood and cognition. However, antipsychotics are generally reserved for individuals with severe or treatment-resistant symptoms due to their potential for side effects, including weight gain, metabolic disturbances, and movement disorders.

Despite their potential benefits, pharmacological interventions have several considerations and limitations in treating dissociative disorders. Firstly, medications primarily target symptoms rather than underlying trauma or attachment disruptions contributing to dissociation, and they may not address the core issues driving dissociative symptoms. Additionally, individual responses to medications can vary widely, and finding the right medication and dosage may require a trial-and-error process. Moreover, medications may have side effects that can impact individuals' quality of life and adherence to treatment, particularly in the long term. It's essential for healthcare providers to monitor individuals closely for adverse effects and adjust treatment plans accordingly to minimize risks and maximize benefits.

Furthermore, pharmacological interventions should be integrated within a comprehensive treatment approach that includes psychotherapy, psychosocial support, and holistic interventions to address the complex and multifaceted nature of dissociative disorders. Medications should not be used as a standalone treatment but rather as part of a multidimensional treatment plan tailored to each individual's needs, preferences, and treatment goals. By combining pharmacotherapy with psychotherapy and other evidence-based interventions, clinicians can optimize outcomes and promote holistic healing and recovery for individuals affected by dissociative disorders.

Integrative Approaches to Treatment

Integrative approaches to treatment offer a comprehensive and personalized approach to addressing dissociative disorders, recognizing the complex interplay of biological, psychological, and social factors contributing to symptoms. These approaches involve combining multiple treatment modalities, such as pharmacotherapy, psychotherapy, and holistic interventions, to address the diverse needs and challenges of individuals with dissociative disorders. By integrating complementary techniques and interventions, clinicians can target symptoms from multiple angles, enhance treatment efficacy, and promote holistic healing and recovery.

Combining pharmacotherapy with psychotherapy is a cornerstone of integrative treatment for dissociative disorders, as it addresses both the underlying neurobiological dysregulation and the psychological and interpersonal sequelae of trauma. Pharmacotherapy, including antidepressants and antipsychotics, can help alleviate symptoms of depression, anxiety, and mood instability, providing individuals with a stable foundation for engaging in psychotherapeutic work. Psychotherapy, such as cognitive-behavioral therapy (CBT), dialectical behavior therapy (DBT), or Eye Movement Desensitization and Reprocessing (EMDR), helps individuals process traumatic memories, develop coping skills, and integrate dissociated aspects of self-identity. By combining pharmacotherapy to manage symptoms and psychotherapy to address underlying trauma and promote integration, individuals can experience synergistic effects and achieve more sustainable and meaningful recovery outcomes.

Incorporating holistic approaches, such as mindfulness-based practices and body-oriented therapies, further enhances the integrative treatment of dissociative disorders by addressing the mind-body connection and promoting self-regulation and embodiment. Mindfulness practices, such as meditation, breathwork, and body scanning, help individuals cultivate present-moment awareness, reduce reactivity to distressing thoughts and emotions, and foster self-compassion and acceptance. Body-oriented therapies, such as somatic experiencing, sensorimotor psychotherapy, and yoga therapy, focus on integrating traumatic memories stored in the body and promoting somatic awareness and regulation. These approaches help individuals reconnect with their bodily sensations, release tension and trauma held in the body, and develop a sense of safety and empowerment in their physical experience.

Furthermore, integrative approaches to treatment emphasize the importance of addressing environmental and relational factors that may contribute to dissociative symptoms and hinder recovery. Psychosocial support, including family therapy, group therapy, and peer support groups, can provide individuals with validation, empathy, and a sense of belonging, fostering social connectedness and resilience. Additionally, interventions targeting environmental stressors, such as housing instability, financial insecurity, or interpersonal conflict, can help alleviate external stressors that may exacerbate dissociative symptoms and hinder progress in treatment. By addressing the broader context in which dissociative symptoms occur, integrative approaches promote holistic healing and empower individuals to reclaim agency and autonomy in their lives.

In conclusion, integrative approaches to treatment offer a comprehensive and multifaceted approach to addressing dissociative disorders, combining pharmacotherapy, psychotherapy, and holistic interventions to target symptoms from multiple angles. By integrating complementary techniques and addressing the diverse needs and challenges of individuals with dissociation, integrative treatment promotes holistic healing and recovery, empowering individuals to reclaim agency and autonomy in their lives. Through a collaborative and personalized approach, clinicians can optimize treatment outcomes and foster resilience, empowerment, and well-being for individuals affected by dissociative disorders.

Challenges in Treating Dissociative Symptoms

Treating dissociative symptoms presents a myriad of challenges and considerations due to the complex and multifaceted nature of dissociative disorders. One challenge is the variability in symptom presentation and severity among individuals, which can complicate diagnosis and treatment planning. Dissociative symptoms often co-occur with other psychiatric disorders, such as post-traumatic stress disorder (PTSD), depression, and substance abuse, further complicating treatment efforts. Additionally, individuals with dissociative disorders may have a history of trauma, attachment disruptions, and interpersonal difficulties, which can impact their ability to engage in therapy and form trusting therapeutic relationships. Therefore, clinicians must adopt a flexible and individualized approach to treatment, taking into account the unique needs, preferences, and challenges of each client.

Building a therapeutic alliance with dissociative clients is essential for fostering trust, safety, and collaboration in therapy. Individuals with dissociative disorders may have a history of invalidation, betrayal, or relational trauma, making it challenging to establish rapport and trust with therapists. Clinicians must create a safe and supportive therapeutic environment where clients feel validated, respected, and understood. This involves adopting a trauma-informed approach to therapy, emphasizing transparency, predictability, and empowerment, and allowing clients to take an active role in their treatment. By building a strong therapeutic alliance, clinicians can facilitate the exploration, processing, and integration of dissociative symptoms, promoting healing and recovery.

Addressing safety concerns and self-harming behaviors is a critical aspect of treating dissociative symptoms, as individuals with dissociative disorders may be at increased risk of self-harm, suicidality, or risky behaviors. Clinicians must conduct thorough assessments of suicidality, self-harm, and safety risks and develop safety plans collaboratively with clients to mitigate risks and enhance safety. This may involve implementing strategies for emotion regulation, distress tolerance, and crisis management, as well as establishing clear boundaries and guidelines for managing suicidal ideation and self-harming behaviors. Additionally, clinicians must monitor clients closely for signs of escalating distress or imminent risk and intervene promptly to ensure their safety and well-being.

Long-term treatment goals and management of chronic symptoms require a holistic and phased approach that addresses the underlying trauma and attachment disruptions contributing to dissociative symptoms. The overarching goal of treatment is to promote integration and coherence of self-identity, enhance emotion regulation and interpersonal functioning, and improve overall quality of life. This may involve a combination of pharmacotherapy, psychotherapy, and holistic interventions tailored to the unique needs and preferences of each client. Long-term treatment planning also involves establishing realistic expectations for therapy and recognizing that healing from dissociative disorders is often a gradual and nonlinear process that requires patience, persistence, and commitment.

Working with co-occurring disorders, such as PTSD, depression, and substance abuse, requires a comprehensive and integrated approach that addresses the complex interplay of symptoms and comorbidities. Clinicians must assess for and treat co-occurring disorders concurrently with dissociative symptoms, as untreated comorbidities can exacerbate dissociative symptoms and hinder progress in therapy. This may involve adapting evidence-based interventions for specific disorders, addressing underlying trauma and attachment issues, and providing psychoeducation and support for managing symptoms effectively. By addressing co-occurring disorders in tandem with dissociative symptoms, clinicians can optimize treatment outcomes and promote holistic healing and recovery.

The importance of cultural competence and sensitivity in treatment interventions cannot be overstated, as cultural factors play a significant role in shaping individuals' experiences of dissociation and their help-seeking behaviors. Clinicians must be mindful of cultural differences in language, communication styles, beliefs about mental health, and attitudes toward treatment. This involves developing cultural humility, recognizing and challenging biases and assumptions, and engaging in ongoing self-reflection and education to enhance cultural competence. By incorporating culturally sensitive and responsive interventions, clinicians can create inclusive and affirming therapeutic spaces that honor the diversity of human experiences and promote healing and recovery for individuals from diverse cultural backgrounds.

Chapter Seven
Paths to Recovery

Traditional And Unconventional Therapies

Overview Of Traditional Therapies

In the realm of healthcare, traditional therapies encompass a wide array of conventional treatments that have long been pillars of medical practice. Among these, medication, surgery, and physical therapy stand as stalwarts in the arsenal against disease and injury. Medication, often the first line of defense in treating illnesses ranging from infections to chronic conditions like hypertension, operates by targeting specific biological pathways to alleviate symptoms or address underlying causes. While medications have undeniably revolutionized healthcare, their effectiveness can vary depending on individual responses and the nature of the condition being treated. Additionally, concerns regarding side effects, drug interactions, and the potential for dependency underscore the need for judicious prescribing and close monitoring by healthcare providers.

Surgery, another cornerstone of traditional therapy, offers definitive solutions for a myriad of health issues, from removing tumors to repairing traumatic injuries. Its efficacy is often unparalleled in cases where non-invasive or conservative approaches prove inadequate. However, surgical interventions come with inherent risks, including complications such as infections, bleeding, and anesthesia-related issues. Furthermore, not all conditions can be addressed surgically, and post-operative recovery can be lengthy and challenging for patients, necessitating careful consideration of alternative treatment options.

Physical therapy rounds out the triad of traditional therapies, focusing on restoring mobility, strength, and function through targeted exercises, manual techniques, and modalities such as ultrasound and electrical stimulation. Its effectiveness extends across various musculoskeletal and neurological conditions, facilitating rehabilitation after surgeries or injuries and managing chronic pain. Nonetheless, physical therapy's success hinges on patient compliance, motivation, and access to ongoing care, and its impact may be limited in cases of advanced or irreversible impairment.

While traditional therapies have undoubtedly transformed healthcare and saved countless lives, their limitations underscore the need for a multifaceted approach to treatment. Recognizing the individuality of patients and the complex interplay of biological, psychological, and social factors influencing health outcomes is paramount. By integrating conventional treatments with complementary and alternative therapies, harnessing the power of the mind-body connection, and embracing patient-centered care, healthcare providers can strive towards more holistic and personalized approaches to healing. Thus, while traditional therapies remain foundational, the future of medicine lies in embracing innovation and embracing a broader spectrum of healing modalities.

Exploring Alternative Therapies

In recent years, there has been a growing interest in and utilization of complementary and alternative therapies as adjuncts or alternatives to conventional medical treatments. Among these therapies, acupuncture, chiropractic care, and herbal medicine have garnered significant attention for their potential to address a wide range of health concerns. Acupuncture, rooted in traditional Chinese medicine, involves the insertion of thin needles into specific points of the body to stimulate energy flow and restore balance. This practice is believed to regulate the body's vital energy or Qi and has been used for millennia to alleviate pain, reduce inflammation, and promote overall well-being.

Chiropractic care focuses on the musculoskeletal system and the spine's alignment, emphasizing manual adjustments to correct misalignments, known as subluxations, which may impede nerve function and disrupt the body's natural healing processes. By restoring proper spinal alignment and optimizing nervous system function, chiropractic adjustments aim to alleviate pain, improve mobility, and enhance overall health and vitality. Additionally, chiropractors may incorporate complementary modalities such as massage therapy, exercise prescription, and lifestyle counseling to support patients' holistic well-being.

Herbal medicine, encompassing a vast array of botanical remedies, relies on the therapeutic properties of plants to prevent and treat various ailments. Herbal preparations may include teas, tinctures, capsules, or topical formulations, with each herb possessing unique medicinal properties and potential health benefits. From soothing digestive discomfort with peppermint tea to relieving joint pain with turmeric supplements, herbal medicine offers a natural and often gentler alternative to pharmaceuticals, with fewer adverse effects and a rich history of traditional use.

Research supporting the efficacy and safety of these alternative therapies continues to accumulate, bolstering their integration into mainstream healthcare. Numerous clinical studies have demonstrated acupuncture's effectiveness in managing conditions such as chronic pain, migraines, and nausea with minimal risk of adverse effects. Likewise, chiropractic care has been shown to be beneficial for treating musculoskeletal issues, such as low back pain and neck pain, and improving overall spinal health. Herbal medicine, too, has garnered scientific interest, with studies validating the therapeutic potential of botanicals in managing various health conditions, from anxiety and depression to cardiovascular disease and immune support.

While complementary and alternative therapies offer promising avenues for health promotion and disease management, it's essential to approach their utilization with discernment and in conjunction with conventional medical care. Collaborative, integrative approaches that leverage the strengths of both traditional and alternative therapies can provide patients with comprehensive and personalized treatment plans tailored to their unique needs and preferences. By embracing a diverse spectrum of healing modalities and fostering an open dialogue between patients and healthcare providers, we can cultivate a more holistic and patient-centered approach to healthcare that empowers individuals to take an active role in their well-being.

Integrative Approaches

The evolution of healthcare has led to a notable trend towards integrating conventional medical practices with complementary and alternative therapies, giving rise to what is known as integrative medicine. This approach recognizes the interconnectedness of mind, body, and spirit in health and illness, advocating for a holistic approach to healing that addresses not only the physical symptoms but also the emotional, social, and spiritual dimensions of well-being. By combining the best of both worlds—conventional treatments backed by scientific evidence and alternative therapies rooted in traditional healing practices—integrative medicine aims to offer patients a comprehensive and personalized approach to healthcare that acknowledges their individual needs and preferences.

Across the globe, hospitals and clinics are embracing integrative medicine programs to meet the growing demand for holistic healthcare options. These programs often encompass a wide range of services, including acupuncture, chiropractic care, massage therapy, nutritional counseling, mindfulness-based stress reduction, and yoga. Examples of leading healthcare institutions pioneering integrative medicine initiatives include the Cleveland Clinic, Mayo Clinic, and University of California, San Francisco (UCSF) Medical Center, among others. These institutions not only provide access to a diverse array of integrative therapies but also conduct research to evaluate their effectiveness and safety, contributing to the growing body of evidence supporting integrative approaches to health and wellness.

Central to the success of integrative medicine is the principle of patient-centered care, which emphasizes collaboration between patients and healthcare providers in decision-making and treatment planning. In choosing the right therapies, it is essential to consider each patient's unique needs, values, beliefs, and preferences, as well as their medical history, diagnosis, and treatment goals. By engaging patients as active participants in their care and respecting their autonomy and choices, healthcare providers can foster trust, empowerment, and better treatment outcomes. Moreover, patient-centered care encourages a more holistic understanding of health, acknowledging the interconnectedness of physical, emotional, and spiritual well-being and the importance of addressing the root causes of illness.

In navigating the complex landscape of integrative medicine, healthcare providers play a crucial role in guiding patients toward evidence-based therapies while respecting their preferences and cultural backgrounds. This may involve providing education and resources to help patients make informed decisions, facilitating open and honest communication, and collaborating with a multidisciplinary team of practitioners to develop comprehensive treatment plans. Additionally, ongoing research and evaluation are essential to continually refine and improve integrative medicine practices, ensuring that they remain safe, effective, and aligned with the evolving needs of patients and society.

As the paradigm of healthcare continues to shift towards a more holistic and patient-centered approach, integrative medicine offers a promising framework for addressing the diverse and complex healthcare needs of individuals and communities. By embracing the integration of conventional and alternative therapies, promoting patient-centered care, and fostering collaboration between patients and healthcare providers, we can move towards a healthcare system that not only treats disease but also promotes optimal health and well-being across the lifespan.

The Mind-Body Connection in Healing

Understanding The Mind-Body Connection

The intricate relationship between the mind and body forms the cornerstone of psychosomatic medicine, a field that examines how mental and emotional factors influence physical health. Psychosomatic medicine recognizes that the mind and body are interconnected systems, with each exerting a profound influence on the other. This holistic perspective challenges the traditional dichotomy between physical and mental health, highlighting the dynamic interplay between psychological well-being and physiological functioning. Through this lens, psychosomatic medicine elucidates the mechanisms by which emotions, thoughts, and behaviors can impact the onset, progression, and resolution of illness.

Stress, in particular, plays a pivotal role in the mind-body connection, serving as a potent trigger for a wide range of physiological responses. When the body perceives a threat or challenge, whether real or perceived, it initiates the stress response, activating the sympathetic nervous system and releasing stress hormones such as cortisol and adrenaline. While this response is adaptive in the short term, chronic or excessive stress can have detrimental effects on physical health, contributing to a host of conditions, including cardiovascular disease, immune dysfunction, gastrointestinal disorders, and mental health disorders such as anxiety and depression.

Emotions, too, exert a profound influence on health outcomes, shaping our perceptions, behaviors, and physiological responses. Positive emotions such as joy, love, and gratitude have been linked to improved immune function, cardiovascular health, and overall well-being, whereas negative emotions such as anger, fear, and sadness can increase susceptibility to illness and exacerbate existing health problems. Moreover, the beliefs and attitudes we hold about ourselves, our health, and the world around us can profoundly impact our health behaviors and outcomes. The placebo effect, for example, demonstrates the powerful influence of belief and expectation on treatment efficacy, with individuals experiencing symptom relief or improvement in health outcomes simply by believing that a treatment is effective.

In understanding the mind-body connection, it becomes evident that mental and emotional factors play a pivotal role in shaping our health and well-being. By recognizing the complex interplay between psychological and physiological processes, healthcare providers can adopt more holistic approaches to patient care that address the underlying drivers of illness and promote healing and resilience. Incorporating strategies to manage stress, cultivate positive emotions, and challenge maladaptive beliefs can empower individuals to optimize their health and mitigate the impact of psychosocial factors on disease. Moreover, fostering supportive relationships, promoting self-awareness, and facilitating mindfulness practices can enhance resilience and promote overall wellness in the face of life's challenges.

Mind-Body Practices

Mind-body practices encompass a diverse array of techniques and disciplines that unite the mind and body to promote holistic well-being. Among the most widely recognized practices are meditation, yoga, and tai chi, each offering unique pathways to relaxation, stress reduction, and enhanced overall health. Meditation, originating from ancient contemplative traditions, involves the cultivation of mindfulness and awareness through focused attention or open monitoring of thoughts, sensations, and emotions. Yoga, an ancient Indian practice, combines physical postures, breathwork, and meditation to harmonize the body, mind, and spirit. Tai chi, rooted in Chinese martial arts, emphasizes slow, flowing movements coordinated with deep breathing and mental focus to cultivate balance, flexibility, and inner peace.

These mind-body practices promote relaxation and stress reduction by eliciting the body's relaxation response, a physiological state characterized by decreased heart rate, blood pressure, and muscle tension, and increased parasympathetic nervous system activity. Through deep breathing, mindfulness, and gentle movement, individuals engage the body's innate capacity for self-regulation and relaxation, counteracting the physiological effects of chronic stress and promoting a sense of calm, clarity, and equanimity. Furthermore, mind-body practices enhance overall well-being by fostering greater self-awareness, emotional resilience, and adaptive coping strategies, empowering individuals to navigate life's challenges with greater ease and grace.

Scientific research supports the myriad benefits of mind-body practices for various health conditions, ranging from mental health disorders to chronic medical conditions. Studies have demonstrated the effectiveness of meditation in reducing symptoms of anxiety, depression, post-traumatic stress disorder (PTSD), and insomnia, as well as improving attention, cognitive function, and emotional regulation. Similarly, yoga has been shown to alleviate symptoms of chronic pain, improve flexibility, strength, and balance, and enhance mood and quality of life in individuals with conditions such as arthritis, fibromyalgia, and multiple sclerosis. Tai chi, too, has garnered empirical support for its ability to improve balance, reduce falls, enhance mobility in older adults, and alleviate symptoms of chronic pain, hypertension, and anxiety.

The growing body of scientific evidence supporting the benefits of mind-body practices underscores their potential as valuable adjuncts to conventional medical treatments, offering safe, accessible, and cost-effective approaches to promoting health and well-being. Integrating mind-body practices into healthcare settings, such as hospitals, clinics, and community centers, can expand access to these transformative practices and empower individuals to take an active role in their health and healing. Moreover, fostering interdisciplinary collaborations between healthcare providers, researchers, and mind-body practitioners can advance our understanding of the mechanisms underlying the therapeutic effects of these practices and optimize their integration into clinical care. Ultimately, by embracing mind-body practices as integral components of holistic healthcare, we can cultivate a culture of wellness that honors the interconnectedness of body, mind, and spirit and fosters optimal health and flourishing for all.

Biofeedback And Neurofeedback

Biofeedback and neurofeedback techniques offer innovative approaches to help individuals regulate physiological processes by providing real-time information about bodily functions that are typically outside of conscious awareness. Biofeedback involves monitoring various physiological parameters, such as heart rate, breathing patterns, muscle tension, and skin temperature, and providing feedback to individuals through visual or auditory cues. By learning to interpret and modify these signals, individuals can gain greater control over their bodily functions, leading to improvements in physical and mental health. Similarly, neurofeedback, also known as EEG biofeedback, focuses on measuring and training brainwave activity to enhance self-regulation and optimize brain functioning.

These techniques have demonstrated considerable promise in managing a wide range of conditions, including chronic pain, anxiety, and attention disorders. In chronic pain management, biofeedback can help individuals learn relaxation techniques and reduce muscle tension, thereby alleviating pain and improving overall quality of life. By providing individuals with a greater sense of control over their physiological responses, biofeedback can empower them to cope more effectively with pain and reduce reliance on medication. Similarly, biofeedback has been used successfully in the treatment of anxiety disorders, enabling individuals to identify and modulate stress responses, regulate breathing patterns, and cultivate a sense of calm and relaxation in challenging situations.

Neurofeedback holds particular relevance in the management of attention disorders such as attention-deficit/hyperactivity disorder (ADHD). By training individuals to modulate their brainwave patterns, particularly in regions associated with attention and impulse control, neurofeedback can enhance cognitive function, improve sustained attention, and reduce hyperactivity and impulsivity. This non-invasive and drug-free approach offers a promising alternative or adjunct to traditional treatments for ADHD, with research suggesting sustained improvements in attention and behavior following neurofeedback training.

Numerous case studies and clinical trials have highlighted the effectiveness of biofeedback and neurofeedback techniques in improving health outcomes across various populations and conditions. For example, a case study published in the Journal of Neurotherapy documented significant reductions in migraine frequency and intensity following neurofeedback training targeting abnormal brainwave patterns associated with migraines. Similarly, a randomized controlled trial published in the Journal of Attention Disorders found that children with ADHD who received neurofeedback training showed significant improvements in attention, behavior, and academic performance compared to those who received stimulant medication or placebo.

Overall, biofeedback and neurofeedback techniques offer safe, non-invasive, and personalized approaches to improving health and well-being by harnessing the power of self-regulation and neuroplasticity. As our understanding of the mind-body connection continues to evolve, these innovative therapies hold promise for addressing the underlying mechanisms of various health conditions and empowering individuals to take an active role in their healing journey. By integrating biofeedback and neurofeedback into mainstream healthcare settings and promoting further research and development in this field, we can expand access to these transformative therapies and optimize their effectiveness in promoting optimal health and flourishing for all.

Case Studies and Patient Stories

Personal Narratives

Personal narratives offer profound insights into the human experience of illness, resilience, and recovery, shedding light on the diverse paths individuals traverse in their journey toward healing. One such narrative is that of Sarah, who battled chronic pain for years following a car accident. Faced with limited mobility and debilitating pain, Sarah explored various treatment options, from conventional medications to physical therapy and acupuncture. Despite setbacks and moments of despair, Sarah persevered, drawing strength from her support network and inner resilience. Through a combination of treatments tailored to her needs, Sarah gradually regained function and found relief, reclaiming her quality of life and inspiring others with her journey of resilience and hope.

Similarly, the story of James highlights the challenges individuals with mental health disorders encounter and the transformative power of holistic approaches to healing. Struggling with severe anxiety and depression, James felt overwhelmed by intrusive thoughts and emotional turmoil. Conventional treatments provided some relief but fell short of addressing the underlying causes of his symptoms. Desperate for relief, James turned to mindfulness meditation, yoga, and therapy, embracing a holistic approach to mental health. Through dedicated practice and self-reflection, James learned to manage his anxiety and depression, cultivating greater self-awareness, acceptance, and inner peace. Today, James serves as a beacon of hope for others navigating similar struggles, advocating for a compassionate and integrative approach to mental health care.

Another compelling narrative is that of Maria, who confronted the challenges of addiction and recovery with courage and determination. Caught in a cycle of substance abuse for years, Maria faced numerous obstacles on her path to sobriety, including withdrawal symptoms, cravings, and social stigma. Despite the odds, Maria sought help and embarked on a journey of recovery, enrolling in a comprehensive treatment program that addressed the physical, emotional, and spiritual dimensions of addiction. With the support of peers, counselors, and loved ones, Maria learned to confront her past traumas, develop healthy coping mechanisms, and rebuild her life free from addiction. Today, Maria celebrates her sobriety and serves as a source of inspiration for others striving to overcome addiction and reclaim their autonomy and dignity.

These personal narratives underscore the resilience of the human spirit and the transformative potential of personalized and holistic approaches to healing. By sharing their stories, individuals like Sarah, James, and Maria illuminate the challenges and triumphs of the healing journey, offering hope and encouragement to others facing similar struggles. Their experiences remind us of the importance of compassion, empathy, and support in navigating life's adversities and reaffirm the power of the human connection in fostering healing and growth. As we listen to and honor these personal narratives, we gain a deeper understanding of the complexity of human suffering and resilience, inspiring us to cultivate greater empathy, solidarity, and compassion in our quest for healing and well-being.

Diverse Perspectives

Diverse perspectives in the realm of healing encompass a multitude of experiences, reflecting the rich tapestry of humanity's journey toward wellness. One such perspective is that of Aisha, a young woman from a low-income neighborhood who grappled with chronic health issues. Despite facing financial barriers and limited access to healthcare, Aisha demonstrated remarkable resilience and resourcefulness in seeking solutions to her health challenges. Through community resources, telehealth services, and advocacy efforts, Aisha navigated the complexities of the healthcare system and pursued alternative therapies such as herbal medicine and meditation to manage her symptoms. Her story highlights the resilience and determination of individuals facing socioeconomic disparities in accessing healthcare, as well as the importance of community support and empowerment in overcoming barriers to healing.

Conversely, the story of Carlos, a middle-aged man from a culturally diverse background, sheds light on the impact of cultural beliefs and practices on treatment choices and outcomes. Growing up in a family steeped in traditional healing modalities, Carlos sought holistic approaches to managing his chronic pain and anxiety. Drawing upon his cultural heritage, Carlos incorporated rituals, ceremonies, and herbal remedies into his healing journey, finding solace and strength in reconnecting with his roots. Despite facing skepticism from mainstream healthcare providers, Carlos remained steadfast in his belief in the interconnectedness of mind, body, and spirit, ultimately achieving improvements in his physical and emotional well-being. His story underscores the importance of cultural competence and sensitivity in healthcare delivery, as well as the value of honoring diverse healing traditions and perspectives.

In addition to socioeconomic and cultural factors, access to healthcare plays a pivotal role in shaping treatment choices and outcomes for individuals navigating the healing journey. Consider the case of Maria, a single mother living in a rural area with limited healthcare resources. Diagnosed with a chronic illness, Maria faced significant challenges in accessing specialized care and treatments due to geographical barriers and lack of transportation. Despite these obstacles, Maria sought creative solutions, including telemedicine consultations, online support groups, and home-based therapies, to manage her condition and improve her quality of life. Her story underscores the importance of addressing healthcare disparities and ensuring equitable access to services for all individuals, regardless of geographical location or socioeconomic status.

Furthermore, the intersectionality of identity—such as race, gender, sexual orientation, and disability—shapes individuals' experiences of health and healing in profound ways. For example, the story of Malik, a transgender man navigating hormone therapy and gender-affirming care, illustrates the unique challenges and barriers faced by marginalized communities in accessing culturally competent and affirming healthcare services. Malik's journey highlights the importance of inclusive and affirming healthcare practices that recognize and respect individuals' identities, experiences, and needs. By amplifying diverse voices and experiences in the discourse on healing, we can foster greater empathy, understanding, and inclusivity in healthcare delivery, ultimately promoting better health outcomes and well-being for all.

Lessons Learned

Patient stories offer invaluable insights and lessons that illuminate the human experience of illness, resilience, and healing. Through these narratives, several key lessons emerge, shedding light on the universal truths and enduring qualities that shape the healing journey. One such lesson is the power of resilience—the ability to bounce back from adversity, overcome challenges, and adapt to life's uncertainties. Across diverse backgrounds and circumstances, individuals like Sarah, James, and Maria exemplify resilience in the face of adversity, demonstrating courage, determination, and resourcefulness in navigating their health challenges and reclaiming their well-being. Their stories remind us of the inherent strength and resilience within each of us, capable of weathering life's storms and emerging stronger and more resilient than before.

Furthermore, patient stories underscore the transformative potential of empowerment—the process of gaining control, agency, and autonomy in one's health and healing journey. Through their experiences, individuals like Aisha, Carlos, and Malik demonstrate the power of self-advocacy, informed decision-making, and active participation in healthcare decisions. By taking ownership of their health and embracing holistic approaches to healing, they reclaim agency and empowerment, empowering themselves to shape their own narratives and pursue paths to wellness aligned with their values and beliefs. Their stories highlight the importance of empowering individuals as partners in their care, fostering collaboration, respect, and dignity in healthcare relationships.

Moreover, patient stories underscore the critical role of support networks—comprising family, friends, healthcare providers, and community resources—in facilitating healing and recovery. Whether it's the unwavering support of loved ones, the guidance of compassionate healthcare providers, or the camaraderie of peer support groups, individuals like Maria, Carlos, and Malik benefit from the strength and solidarity of their support networks. These networks provide emotional support, practical assistance, and invaluable resources, bolstering individuals' resilience and fostering a sense of belonging and connection amidst life's challenges. Their stories remind us of the profound impact of social support in promoting health and well-being, underscoring the importance of fostering supportive and inclusive communities that uplift and empower individuals on their healing journey.

Additionally, patient stories emphasize the importance of holistic approaches to healing that address the interconnectedness of mind, body, and spirit. Through their experiences, individuals like James and Maria illustrate the transformative power of integrating conventional and alternative therapies, cultivating mindfulness and self-awareness, and nurturing the mind-body connection. By embracing a holistic perspective that honors the multifaceted nature of health and well-being, individuals can tap into their innate capacity for healing and resilience, fostering greater harmony, balance, and vitality in their lives. Their stories inspire us to adopt a more comprehensive and integrative approach to healthcare, one that acknowledges the interplay of biological, psychological, social, and spiritual factors in shaping health outcomes.

In conclusion, patient stories offer profound lessons and insights into the human experience of illness, resilience, and healing. Through their narratives, we learn about the transformative power of resilience, empowerment, and support networks in navigating life's challenges and reclaiming well-being. By extracting key lessons and common themes from these stories, we gain a deeper understanding of the universal truths and enduring qualities that shape the healing journey, inspiring us to foster greater resilience, empowerment, and community support in our quest for health and well-being.

Chapter Eight
Trauma and Society

The Broader Implications of
Trauma on Communities and Societies

Community Resilience

Community resilience serves as a vital mechanism in navigating the profound impact of trauma on the fabric of communities. When trauma strikes, whether through natural disasters, acts of violence, or other collective tragedies, the very essence of community cohesion can be deeply shaken. The sense of safety and belonging that once defined these communities may be fractured, leading to widespread emotional distress and social upheaval. Individuals within these communities often grapple with heightened levels of anxiety, fear, and grief, which can strain interpersonal relationships and erode trust. Furthermore, economic disparities and systemic inequalities may exacerbate the trauma's effects, disproportionately affecting marginalized groups within the community.

However, amidst the devastation, communities often exhibit remarkable resilience, drawing upon various internal and external resources to mitigate the trauma's impact. Resilience factors such as social cohesion, solidarity, and a shared sense of purpose play a crucial role in buffering against the adverse effects of trauma. Strong social networks and support systems provide avenues for individuals to seek comfort, share experiences, and rebuild connections, fostering a collective resilience that transcends individual suffering. Additionally, community organizations, religious institutions, and grassroots initiatives often mobilize to provide practical assistance, emotional support, and spaces for healing, amplifying the community's resilience in the face of adversity.

Numerous case studies offer poignant examples of communities rallying together in response to collective trauma, showcasing the power of resilience in action. In the aftermath of natural disasters like hurricanes, earthquakes, or wildfires, affected communities frequently demonstrate remarkable resilience as they come together to rebuild homes, infrastructure, and livelihoods. Likewise, in instances of mass violence or societal unrest, communities often unite in solidarity to advocate for justice, promote healing, and prevent future tragedies. These collective efforts not only facilitate recovery but also foster a sense of empowerment and agency among community members, reinforcing their resilience in the face of ongoing challenges.

For instance, following the devastating impact of Hurricane Katrina in 2005, the city of New Orleans faced widespread destruction and displacement. However, the community's resilience was evident in the grassroots initiatives, volunteer efforts, and cultural revitalization projects that emerged in the years following the disaster. Similarly, in the wake of the 9/11 terrorist attacks, communities across the United States and around the world came together to offer support, solidarity, and resilience in the face of unimaginable loss and trauma. These examples underscore the importance of nurturing community resilience as a foundational element in responding to and recovering from collective trauma, highlighting the transformative power of solidarity, compassion, and collective action.

Interpersonal Dynamics

Interpersonal dynamics play a crucial role in both the propagation and mitigation of trauma within social networks. When an individual experiences trauma, whether it be from personal tragedy or a shared community event, the effects reverberate through their social connections like ripples in a pond. Close relationships, such as family, friends, and colleagues, may directly witness the aftermath of trauma, experiencing secondary stress and emotional burdens as they support the affected individual. Moreover, the trauma can spread beyond immediate relationships, impacting broader social networks through shared narratives, empathetic responses, and collective mourning. These ripple effects underscore the interconnectedness of human experience and highlight the pervasive influence of trauma on interpersonal dynamics.

The experience of trauma often disrupts social cohesion and erodes trust within communities. Individuals may withdraw from social interactions, isolate themselves from loved ones, or struggle to communicate their feelings and needs effectively. This breakdown in communication and connection can lead to feelings of alienation, misunderstanding, and resentment among community members, further exacerbating the trauma's impact. Moreover, the rupture of trust, whether due to direct harm or perceived betrayal, can undermine the foundation of relationships and fragment the social fabric, leaving individuals feeling vulnerable and unsupported.

Despite the challenges posed by trauma, healing often begins through community engagement and support. Communities have a unique capacity to provide a sense of belonging, validation, and solidarity to those who have experienced trauma. Through collective rituals, storytelling, and shared expressions of empathy, individuals find solace in the company of others who understand their pain and share their journey of recovery. Community-based support groups, peer counseling, and advocacy organizations offer valuable resources and spaces for individuals to process their experiences, rebuild trust, and reclaim their sense of agency. Additionally, acts of kindness, compassion, and mutual aid within the community foster a culture of resilience and hope, reinforcing the bonds that unite individuals in times of adversity.

For example, in the aftermath of a natural disaster, neighbors may come together to provide shelter, supplies, and emotional support to those affected, transcending differences and fostering a sense of unity in the face of adversity. Similarly, in marginalized communities disproportionately impacted by systemic trauma, grassroots movements and solidarity networks often emerge to address underlying social injustices and advocate for collective healing and empowerment. These examples illustrate the transformative potential of community engagement and support in promoting resilience, restoring social cohesion, and facilitating the healing process in the aftermath of trauma.

Economic Consequences

The economic consequences of trauma are multifaceted, with significant implications for both individual productivity and broader economic stability. When individuals experience trauma, whether through personal adversity or collective tragedy, their ability to participate in the workforce may be compromised. Symptoms such as anxiety, depression, and post-traumatic stress disorder (PTSD) can impair cognitive function, concentration, and decision-making, leading to decreased productivity and absenteeism in the workplace. Moreover, the long-term psychological effects of trauma may hinder individuals' career advancement opportunities, perpetuating economic hardship and exacerbating disparities in income and wealth.

In addition to the direct impact on individual productivity, trauma-related healthcare costs impose a substantial burden on both individuals and society as a whole. The physical and mental health consequences of trauma often necessitate medical treatment, therapy, and medication, which can result in significant out-of-pocket expenses for individuals and families. Furthermore, the high demand for mental health services following traumatic events may strain healthcare systems, leading to longer wait times, limited access to specialized care, and increased costs for providers and insurers. As a result, individuals may face financial barriers to accessing necessary care, exacerbating their distress and prolonging their recovery process.

The long-term economic implications of trauma extend beyond the immediate aftermath of the event, profoundly impacting affected communities for years to come. In addition to the direct costs of healthcare and lost productivity, communities may experience declines in property values, business closures, and decreased consumer spending following a traumatic event. Furthermore, the disruption of social networks, loss of trust in institutions, and increased crime rates can impede community development efforts and deter investment in affected areas. Over time, these economic challenges can perpetuate cycles of poverty and social inequality, exacerbating the trauma's impact on vulnerable populations and hindering the community's ability to recover and thrive.

For example, communities devastated by natural disasters such as hurricanes, earthquakes, or wildfires often face long-term economic hardship as they rebuild infrastructure, homes, and businesses. The financial strain of reconstruction efforts, coupled with the loss of tourism revenue and disruption of local industries, can prolong the recovery process and impede economic recovery. Similarly, communities affected by acts of violence or mass trauma may struggle to attract businesses and investment due to safety concerns and negative perceptions, further exacerbating economic disparities and social fragmentation. These examples underscore the far-reaching economic consequences of trauma and highlight the importance of comprehensive support systems and targeted interventions to facilitate recovery and promote resilience in affected communities.

Political And Governance Challenges

The impact of trauma on political stability and governance is profound, as it can exacerbate existing tensions, undermine trust in institutions, and challenge the legitimacy of governing bodies. In times of crisis or collective trauma, political leaders may face increased scrutiny and pressure to respond effectively, maintain social order, and address the needs of affected populations. However, the very nature of trauma, with its potential to disrupt social cohesion and incite fear and uncertainty, poses significant challenges to governance structures. Political instability may arise as communities grapple with the aftermath of traumatic events, leading to heightened social unrest, protests, and even political upheaval. Moreover, the erosion of trust in government institutions can further weaken the social contract between rulers and citizens, exacerbating existing governance challenges and undermining democratic processes.

Handling trauma in the context of conflict and post-conflict societies presents unique challenges, as historical grievances, intergroup tensions, and ongoing violence complicate the recovery process. In conflict-affected regions, trauma is often pervasive, with entire communities experiencing the devastating consequences of violence, displacement, and loss. Healing and reconciliation efforts must contend with deep-seated mistrust, intergenerational trauma, and competing narratives of victimhood and culpability. Moreover, political actors may exploit trauma to justify continued conflict, perpetuate cycles of violence, and consolidate power, further complicating peacebuilding and conflict resolution efforts. Addressing trauma in post-conflict societies requires a multifaceted approach that prioritizes truth-telling, justice, and inclusive dialogue while addressing the root causes of conflict and promoting social cohesion.

Government responses to large-scale trauma events play a crucial role in shaping the trajectory of recovery and resilience within affected communities. Effective governance requires proactive measures to mitigate the immediate impact of trauma, provide essential services and support to survivors, and facilitate long-term healing and recovery. This may involve deploying emergency response teams, mobilizing resources for humanitarian aid and medical assistance, and coordinating with international partners to ensure a coordinated and comprehensive response. Moreover, governments must prioritize the mental health and well-being of affected populations, investing in trauma-informed care, psychosocial support services, and community-based interventions to promote healing and resilience.

For example, following the 2011 earthquake and tsunami in Japan, the government implemented a range of measures to support affected communities, including temporary housing, financial assistance, and mental health services. Similarly, in the aftermath of terrorist attacks or mass shootings, governments often mobilize crisis response teams, establish victim support funds, and implement security measures to reassure the public and prevent further harm. However, government responses to trauma events are not always effective or equitable, and marginalized communities may face barriers to accessing support and resources. Addressing these disparities requires a commitment to social justice, equity, and human rights, ensuring that all individuals and communities receive the assistance and protection they need to recover and rebuild in the wake of trauma.

Sociocultural Factors in Trauma Response and Recovery

Cultural Norms and Beliefs

Cultural norms and beliefs play a significant role in shaping how individuals perceive and respond to trauma. Across different cultures, there are varying understandings of what constitutes trauma, how it is experienced, and how it should be addressed. Cultural beliefs about the causes of trauma, such as divine punishment, fate, or ancestral curses, influence perceptions of personal responsibility and resilience. Moreover, cultural frameworks shape the expression and interpretation of trauma symptoms, with some cultures emphasizing somatic complaints or spiritual distress over psychological distress. Cultural narratives and symbols also shape how trauma is processed and communicated within communities, influencing coping mechanisms, help-seeking behaviors, and social support networks.

In many cultures, there exists a pervasive stigma surrounding mental health issues, including trauma-related conditions such as PTSD, depression, and anxiety. Cultural taboos against discussing personal struggles or seeking professional help may prevent individuals from accessing the care and support they need. Moreover, cultural attitudes towards mental illness may contribute to feelings of shame, guilt, and self-blame among those experiencing trauma symptoms, leading to social isolation and reluctance to disclose their experiences. The stigma surrounding mental health can be particularly pronounced in collectivist cultures where individual well-being is closely linked to family honor and societal expectations, further complicating efforts to address trauma-related concerns.

Culturally competent approaches to trauma recovery recognize the diversity of cultural beliefs, values, and practices that shape individuals' experiences and responses to trauma. These approaches prioritize cultural humility, empathy, and respect for diverse worldviews, acknowledging that one size does not fit all when it comes to trauma healing. Culturally competent practitioners strive to create safe and inclusive spaces for individuals to explore their trauma narratives, drawing upon cultural strengths, traditions, and resources to facilitate healing and resilience. This may involve integrating indigenous healing practices, rituals, and ceremonies into treatment modalities, collaborating with community leaders and healers, and adapting evidence-based interventions to align with cultural norms and preferences.

For example, in indigenous communities, trauma recovery may involve reconnecting with traditional cultural practices such as storytelling, drumming, or sweat lodge ceremonies, which provide opportunities for healing, reflection, and community support. Similarly, in immigrant and refugee populations, trauma recovery efforts may incorporate culturally specific interventions such as language interpretation, cultural brokering, and trauma-informed resettlement services. By recognizing and respecting cultural diversity, culturally competent approaches to trauma recovery empower individuals to reclaim their narratives, rebuild social connections, and cultivate resilience within their cultural contexts. Ultimately, promoting cultural competence in trauma care is essential for addressing the complex interplay between culture, trauma, and mental health and ensuring that all individuals have access to culturally responsive and equitable support services.

Social Support Networks

Social support networks serve as essential lifelines for individuals navigating the aftermath of trauma, providing comfort, validation, and practical assistance during times of distress. Within these networks, family, community, and cultural ties play a pivotal role in buffering against the adverse effects of trauma and facilitating recovery. Family members often serve as primary sources of emotional support, offering love, understanding, and companionship to those who have experienced trauma. Likewise, close-knit communities and cultural networks provide a sense of belonging, solidarity, and shared identity, fostering a collective resilience that transcends individual suffering. These social connections offer opportunities for individuals to express their emotions, seek guidance, and access resources, strengthening their capacity to cope with trauma and rebuild their lives.

However, despite the benefits of social support networks, there are often significant barriers to seeking and receiving assistance, particularly for individuals affected by trauma. The stigma surrounding mental health issues, cultural taboos against discussing personal struggles, and fear of judgment or rejection may deter individuals from reaching out for help. Moreover, systemic barriers such as limited access to affordable healthcare, language barriers, and discrimination can further isolate trauma survivors and impede their ability to access support services. Additionally, individuals may internalize feelings of shame, self-blame, or worthlessness, which can prevent them from disclosing their experiences or seeking assistance from others.

Strengthening social support systems for trauma survivors requires a multifaceted approach that addresses both individual and systemic barriers to seeking and receiving assistance. Education and awareness campaigns can help reduce the stigma surrounding mental health and trauma, encouraging open dialogue and destigmatizing help-seeking behaviors. Culturally competent services that respect and honor diverse beliefs, values, and traditions can increase accessibility and relevance for marginalized communities. Additionally, community-based interventions such as support groups, peer counseling, and community outreach programs provide spaces for individuals to connect with others who share similar experiences, fostering a sense of solidarity and mutual support.

For example, survivor-led support groups for victims of domestic violence or sexual assault offer opportunities for individuals to share their stories, receive validation, and access resources for safety and healing. Likewise, community-based organizations and grassroots initiatives may provide practical assistance such as transportation, childcare, and housing support to individuals in need. By strengthening social support networks and addressing barriers to assistance, communities can play a vital role in promoting resilience, fostering recovery, and empowering trauma survivors to reclaim their lives and thrive. Ultimately, building a culture of compassion, empathy, and solidarity is essential for creating supportive environments where individuals feel safe, valued, and connected, even in the face of adversity.

Identity And Trauma

Trauma has a profound impact on both individual and collective identity, reshaping how individuals perceive themselves and their place in the world. When someone experiences trauma, whether it's through personal adversity or shared community tragedy, it can fundamentally alter their sense of self, values, and beliefs. Trauma may disrupt the continuity of one's life story, causing individuals to question their identity, purpose, and worth. Moreover, trauma can fragment the cohesive narrative of collective identity within communities, challenging shared beliefs, values, and norms. Individuals may struggle to reconcile their past experiences with their present reality, leading to feelings of alienation, disconnection, and existential crisis as they grapple with the aftermath of trauma.

Cultural narratives of resilience and survival play a crucial role in shaping how individuals and communities respond to trauma and rebuild their identity in its aftermath. Across diverse cultures and societies, there are often stories, myths, and legends that celebrate acts of courage, perseverance, and triumph in the face of adversity. These cultural narratives provide frameworks for understanding and interpreting trauma, offering symbols of hope, strength, and resilience to those who have experienced hardship. Drawing upon cultural traditions, rituals, and wisdom, individuals and communities find solace and inspiration in stories of survival, resilience, and renewal, guiding their journey of healing and identity reconstruction.

Rebuilding identity after trauma is a complex and often nonlinear process that involves integrating the traumatic experience into one's sense of self and creating a new narrative of resilience and growth. Individuals may engage in introspection, reflection, and meaning-making as they seek to make sense of their trauma and its impact on their identity. This process may involve acknowledging and accepting the reality of the trauma, grieving losses, and reclaiming agency and empowerment in their lives. Moreover, individuals may draw upon internal and external resources, such as social support networks, therapy, and spiritual practices, to navigate the challenges of identity reconstruction and find meaning and purpose in their experiences.

For example, survivors of trauma may engage in therapeutic interventions such as narrative therapy or expressive arts therapy to explore and reinterpret their personal narrative in the context of trauma. Similarly, communities affected by collective trauma may engage in collective rituals, memorialization ceremonies, or community-building activities to honor the past, heal collective wounds, and foster a sense of solidarity and resilience. By embracing the complexity of identity reconstruction after trauma, individuals and communities can find strength, meaning, and connection in their shared experiences, ultimately transforming trauma into a catalyst for personal and collective growth.

Cross-Cultural Perspectives

Cross-cultural perspectives on trauma highlight the diverse ways in which individuals and communities around the world respond to and recover from traumatic experiences. Cultural norms, beliefs, and values shape how trauma is perceived, expressed, and addressed within different cultural contexts. Variations in trauma response across cultures may manifest in differences in symptom presentation, coping mechanisms, and help-seeking behaviors. For example, in some cultures, somatic complaints such as headaches or stomachaches may be more commonly reported as expressions of psychological distress, while in others, emotional symptoms such as sadness or anxiety may be more readily acknowledged and expressed. Additionally, cultural factors such as collectivism versus individualism, spiritual beliefs, and the role of social support networks influence how individuals and communities navigate the aftermath of trauma.

Lessons learned from diverse cultural approaches to trauma highlight the importance of recognizing and honoring the unique strengths, resources, and resilience strategies that exist within different cultural contexts. Indigenous healing traditions, spiritual practices, and communal rituals offer valuable insights into alternative pathways to healing and recovery that may complement Western psychological approaches. For example, traditional healing ceremonies, such as sweat lodge ceremonies or vision quests, may provide opportunities for individuals to reconnect with their cultural identity, spiritual beliefs, and community support systems, facilitating healing on multiple levels. Moreover, indigenous models of wellness emphasize holistic approaches to health and well-being that encompass physical, emotional, mental, and spiritual dimensions, challenging dominant biomedical paradigms of trauma treatment and recovery.

Building culturally inclusive trauma interventions requires a commitment to cultural humility, reflexivity, and collaboration with diverse communities to co-create solutions that are sensitive to cultural beliefs, values, and preferences. Culturally competent practitioners recognize the importance of cultural context in shaping individuals' experiences of trauma and prioritize cultural adaptation and tailoring interventions to meet the unique needs of diverse populations. This may involve incorporating culturally relevant metaphors, symbols, and rituals into therapy sessions, providing language interpretation and cultural brokering services, and collaborating with community leaders, healers, and elders to integrate indigenous knowledge and practices into treatment modalities. Moreover, culturally inclusive trauma interventions prioritize empowerment, self-determination, and community engagement, fostering partnerships between practitioners and clients that honor the agency and resilience of trauma survivors.

For example, in immigrant and refugee communities, trauma-informed care models may incorporate trauma-sensitive approaches to language interpretation, culturally specific psychoeducation materials, and community-based support networks to address barriers to care and promote healing. Similarly, in indigenous communities, trauma recovery efforts may involve revitalizing cultural practices, reclaiming traditional healing knowledge, and addressing systemic inequities that contribute to ongoing trauma and intergenerational trauma transmission. By embracing cultural diversity and promoting equity and social justice in trauma care, practitioners and policymakers can create inclusive environments where all individuals and communities have access to the resources and support they need to heal and thrive.

Kenny Ajayi

Necessary Changes in Public Policy and Social Support Systems

Accessible Mental Health Services

Accessible mental health services are critical for addressing the growing demand for mental health care and ensuring that individuals receive timely and effective support for their psychological well-being. However, there are significant gaps in mental health infrastructure that hinder access to care for many people worldwide. Inadequate funding, workforce shortages, and fragmented service delivery systems contribute to long wait times, limited availability of services, and disparities in access based on geographic location, socioeconomic status, and cultural background. Addressing these gaps requires investment in expanding mental health infrastructure, including increasing the number of trained mental health professionals, improving access to psychiatric medications, and enhancing the capacity of existing mental health facilities to meet the diverse needs of the population.

Integrating mental health services into primary care and community settings is essential for improving access and reducing the stigma associated with seeking mental health care. Many individuals seek care for mental health concerns in primary care settings, making it an ideal entry point for early identification and intervention. By integrating mental health screening, assessment, and treatment services into routine primary care visits, healthcare providers can identify and address mental health concerns before they escalate into more serious problems. Moreover, community-based mental health programs, such as peer support groups, counseling centers, and outreach initiatives, provide accessible and culturally sensitive services that meet the needs of diverse populations and promote holistic approaches to mental health and well-being.

Policies to increase access to affordable mental health care are essential for ensuring that individuals can access the services they need without facing financial barriers. This may involve expanding public insurance coverage for mental health services, reducing out-of-pocket costs for mental health care, and implementing reimbursement policies that incentivize providers to offer evidence-based treatments. Additionally, policies aimed at addressing social determinants of mental health, such as poverty, unemployment, and homelessness, can indirectly improve access to care by addressing underlying factors that contribute to mental health disparities. Furthermore, policies that promote telehealth and digital mental health platforms can increase access to care for individuals in remote or underserved areas, as well as those who face mobility or transportation challenges.

For example, countries like Australia and the United Kingdom have implemented policies to increase access to mental health care through initiatives such as the Better Access program and the Improving Access to Psychological Therapies (IAPT) program, respectively. These programs aim to reduce barriers to care by providing subsidized mental health services in primary care settings and community-based clinics. Similarly, in the United States, the Affordable Care Act expanded insurance coverage for mental health services and required parity between mental health and physical health coverage, ensuring that mental health care is accessible and affordable for millions of Americans. By prioritizing policies that improve access to mental health care, policymakers can promote population-wide mental health and well-being and reduce the burden of mental illness on individuals, families, and communities.

Trauma-Informed Education and Training:

Trauma-informed education and training are essential for equipping professionals across various sectors with the knowledge, skills, and sensitivity needed to effectively support individuals who have experienced trauma. This training goes beyond traditional clinical settings to encompass diverse fields such as healthcare, education, law enforcement, social work, and community services. Professionals who interact with trauma survivors must understand the complex interplay of biological, psychological, and social factors that influence trauma responses and recovery. Training programs typically focus on topics such as trauma awareness, trauma-informed assessment and intervention techniques, cultural competency, and self-care strategies to prevent burnout and vicarious traumatization. By providing comprehensive training in trauma-informed care, professionals can create safe and supportive environments that promote healing and resilience for trauma survivors across diverse settings.

Incorporating trauma-informed approaches into education systems is crucial for supporting students who have experienced trauma and creating trauma-sensitive learning environments. Teachers, school counselors, and administrators play a vital role in recognizing the signs of trauma, providing appropriate support, and creating safe spaces where students feel understood and valued. Trauma-informed education emphasizes the importance of building positive relationships, fostering a sense of belonging, and promoting emotional regulation and coping skills among students. Additionally, trauma-informed practices prioritize prevention and early intervention strategies to address trauma-related challenges and promote academic success. By integrating trauma-informed principles into school policies, curriculum development, and staff training, education systems can better meet the diverse needs of students and enhance overall well-being and academic outcomes.

Building awareness of trauma's impact on various sectors of society is essential for promoting empathy, understanding, and action to address the needs of trauma survivors. Training programs and public awareness campaigns can help raise awareness about the prevalence and consequences of trauma across diverse populations and settings. By educating policymakers, community leaders, and the general public about the importance of trauma-informed approaches, advocates can mobilize support for policies and initiatives that prioritize trauma prevention, intervention, and recovery. Additionally, building partnerships between sectors such as healthcare, education, social services, and criminal justice can facilitate cross-disciplinary collaboration and ensure that trauma survivors receive comprehensive and coordinated care that addresses their holistic needs.

For example, initiatives such as the Adverse Childhood Experiences (ACEs) study have raised awareness about the lifelong impact of childhood trauma on health outcomes and social functioning, leading to increased investment in trauma-informed practices in healthcare, education, and other sectors. Similarly, trauma-informed training programs for law enforcement officers have been shown to improve officer interactions with individuals experiencing mental health crises and reduce the use of force in encounters with trauma survivors. By promoting a trauma-informed approach across sectors, communities can create a more compassionate and supportive society that prioritizes the well-being and dignity of all its members, especially those who have experienced trauma.

Legal And Justice System Reforms:

Legal and justice system reforms are essential for creating more equitable and trauma-informed approaches to addressing crime, supporting victims, and promoting rehabilitation and community reintegration. Trauma-informed approaches in law enforcement and judiciary systems recognize the prevalence and impact of trauma among both victims and offenders. This involves training law enforcement officers, judges, and legal professionals to recognize signs of trauma, respond with sensitivity and empathy, and avoid re-traumatizing individuals who come into contact with the justice system. By integrating trauma-informed principles into police practices, court proceedings, and correctional facilities, the legal system can better serve the needs of trauma-affected individuals and reduce the cycle of trauma and re-offending.

Alternatives to incarceration for trauma-affected individuals are gaining recognition as more effective and humane responses to addressing criminal behavior. Rather than punitive measures that exacerbate trauma and perpetuate cycles of violence, trauma-informed interventions prioritize rehabilitation, treatment, and community-based support services. Diversion programs, specialty courts (such as drug courts and mental health courts), restorative justice practices, and community supervision programs offer trauma-affected individuals opportunities for healing, accountability, and skill-building while remaining connected to their families and communities. By providing trauma-informed alternatives to incarceration, the legal system can reduce recidivism rates, alleviate prison overcrowding, and promote the rehabilitation and reintegration of individuals who have experienced trauma.

Victim-centered legal reforms prioritize the rights, needs, and voices of victims of crime, ensuring that they are treated with dignity, respect, and compassion throughout the legal process. This involves implementing policies and practices that empower victims to participate in legal proceedings, access support services, and exercise their rights to safety, restitution, and justice. Victim-centered approaches also involve providing trauma-informed support services, such as counseling, advocacy, and crisis intervention, to help victims cope with the emotional and practical challenges of navigating the legal system. Additionally, legal reforms may include measures to protect victims from secondary victimization, such as harassment, intimidation, and retaliation, and to hold perpetrators accountable for their actions.

Social safety nets encompass a range of policies and programs designed to provide financial, material, and social support to individuals and families facing economic hardship, social exclusion, and other forms of adversity. These safety nets include social assistance programs such as cash transfers, food assistance, and housing subsidies, as well as social insurance programs such as unemployment insurance, disability benefits, and healthcare coverage. By providing a basic level of economic security and social support, social safety nets help prevent individuals and families from falling into poverty and experiencing the associated risks of poor health, educational attainment, and social mobility. Additionally, social safety nets can serve as a buffer against the impact of trauma and adversity, providing individuals with the resources and support they need to cope with life's challenges and rebuild their lives after experiencing trauma.

In summary, legal and justice system reforms that prioritize trauma-informed approaches, alternatives to incarceration, victim-centered practices, and social safety nets are essential for promoting justice, healing, and resilience in communities affected by trauma. By implementing these reforms, policymakers, legal professionals, and community leaders can create more equitable and compassionate systems that support the well-being and dignity of all individuals, especially those who have experienced trauma and adversity.

Prevention And Early Intervention:

Prevention and early intervention strategies are crucial components of a comprehensive approach to addressing trauma and adversity, aiming to reduce the prevalence and severity of traumatic experiences and mitigate their long-term impact on individuals and communities. Implementing programs to prevent trauma and adversity involves addressing underlying risk factors such as poverty, inequality, social exclusion, and violence through targeted interventions and policy reforms. These programs may include initiatives to promote economic opportunity, affordable housing, quality education, access to healthcare, and community safety. By addressing the root causes of trauma and adversity, prevention programs aim to create supportive environments that foster resilience, reduce the incidence of traumatic events, and promote overall well-being.

Early intervention strategies play a vital role in identifying and addressing trauma-related challenges at the earliest possible stage before they escalate into more serious problems. This may involve screening for trauma exposure and related symptoms in healthcare settings, schools, and community organizations to identify individuals who may benefit from early intervention services. Early intervention programs may include mental health services, counseling, case management, and support groups tailored to the needs of trauma-affected individuals and communities. By intervening early, these programs aim to prevent the onset of more severe mental health problems, substance abuse, and other negative outcomes associated with untreated trauma.

Promoting resilience-building initiatives in communities is essential for equipping individuals and communities with the skills, resources, and support networks needed to cope with adversity and bounce back from traumatic experiences. Resilience-building initiatives may include community-based programs, workshops, and training sessions that teach coping skills, stress management techniques, and problem-solving strategies. Additionally, fostering social connections, supportive relationships, and a sense of belonging within communities can enhance resilience and buffer against the impact of trauma. By promoting resilience at the individual, family, and community levels, these initiatives help build a foundation of strength and support that empowers individuals to overcome adversity and thrive in the face of challenges.

For example, school-based resilience programs may teach students skills such as emotional regulation, conflict resolution, and positive communication to help them navigate stressors and build healthy relationships. Similarly, community resilience-building initiatives may involve organizing neighborhood watch programs, creating safe spaces for youth to gather and engage in positive activities, and providing access to mental health and social support services. By fostering resilience and social cohesion within communities, these initiatives strengthen the protective factors that promote well-being and mitigate the impact of trauma and adversity.

In summary, prevention and early intervention strategies are essential components of a comprehensive approach to addressing trauma and adversity. By implementing programs to prevent trauma, intervening early to address trauma-related challenges, and promoting resilience-building initiatives in communities, policymakers, healthcare providers, and community leaders can create supportive environments that promote well-being, prevent future trauma, and empower individuals and communities to overcome adversity and thrive.

Chapter Nine
Conclusion

Summary Of Key Insights

Emphasize The Interconnectedness of Psychological and Physiological Responses:

As long as the link between psychological and physiological reactions to trauma is understood, a certain and holistic approach to treating the consequences of traumatic experiences can be expected. Trauma initiates a long chain of responses in the body and in the mind. Thus, the chemical symptoms of trauma are intertwined with the psychological ones. Emotionally, survivors of a traumatic event may experience symptoms of intrusive thoughts, nightmares, and hypervigilance that are the consequence of the significant disruption it produces on the cognitive and emotional processes. The psychological reactions are mostly accompanied by physiological changes like rapid heart rate, muscle tension, and cortisol level alterations in the stress hormone, amongst others. Recognizing the links between the observable and the invisible appearance of trauma emphasizes the necessity of structural treatment that includes the mental and physical elements of trauma.

Additionally, studies in psycho-neuro-immunology that scientifically explore the intricate relationships among the brain, immune system, and endocrine system in response to trauma have been illuminated. The body's chronic responses to severe and timely emotional events can even set off a maladaptive function in these systems, which might be the origin of long-term health issues such as inflammation, autoimmune disorders, and cardiovascular problems. The limbic system's major parts, i.e., the amygdala and hippocampus, are responsible for trauma and trauma and are the main center of emotion processing. The faults in such brain areas might cause other problems like post-traumatic stress and depression; this effectively shows that there is an interplay between the physiological and psychological responses.

Additionally, learning about the link between emotional and physical responses to trauma assists in the formulation of trauma treatment approaches that deal with both sides. Therapeutic strategies such as cognitive-behavioral therapy (CBT), mindfulness-based stress reduction (MBSR), and somatic experiencing combine techniques to control emotions, change negative thought patterns, and relieve physical tension. These methods are able to deal with psychic discomfort as well as physiological arousal; hence, holistic healing and re-gaining control of life is being empowered by individuals. Stressing the interconnectedness of these responses not only deepens the understanding of trauma but also brings into play the use of evidence-based treatment techniques that meet the specific needs of trauma survivors.

How Trauma Affects Various Systems in The Body?

Trauma, however, wounds the body so profoundly as to subvert and degrade the function of many systems in the body, thus leading to a wide range of physical and psychological symptoms. The latter is made up of the CNS and the PNS, and therefore, it represents the most vulnerable area to the injurious impact of trauma. The SNS is very alert to threats and starts counter-attacks either via the "fight or flight" modifications such as increased heart rate, hyper-arousal, and vigilance. Constant association with trauma upsets this stress response system mode of operation, making an individual demonstrate symptoms of hyperarousal as well as hypervigilance that have been observed in cases of post-traumatic stress disorder (PTSD).

As one more result of the trauma, it can have an impact on the endocrine system, which is the master of the secretion of hormones in the body. The HPA axis, a major element of the endocrine system, links together for the stress response process is the main parts. The impact of trauma is a disruption of the HPA axis and then subsequent cortisol level changes and dysfunction of the system that allows the body to cope with stress. Through dysregulation of the hypothalamic-pituitary-adrenal (HPA) axis, traumatic experiences have been proven to lead to immune depression, endocrine abnormality, and emotional turbulence, a vivid example of the far-reaching nature of psychological injury.

Also, trauma can have a great effect on the immune system, thus making the body less able to generate proper defense, leading to poor health. Chronic stress caused by trauma has a very broad response known as immune dysregulation, which is manifested by increased levels of inflammation and decreases in immune function. Beyond a point, any continued stress response activation implies disturbed production of immunological cells and cytokines; hence, the individuals become more prone to diseases and autoimmune conditions. It also has been reported that post-injury changes in immune function are closely associated with the development of several diseases, such as heart ailments, intestinal disorders, and chronic pain syndromes. Through comprehending how trauma affects these systems within the human body, which interact and impact each other, healthcare providers can create therapy programs that address both the physical and psychological co-occurrence of trauma as they support complete healing and recovery.

The Role of Neuroplasticity

All of the elements that lead to our acceptance of trauma in the brain, neuroplasticity, and the brain's extraordinary potential for reorganization and change in response to experiences stand out as the key. A human mind, during trauma, can experience serious changes related to its structure and functions, mostly in the regions of the brain that are responsible for emotional regulation, memory processing, and stress management. For example, one can imagine that prolonged exposure to experience of trauma may lead to changes in the structure of the amygdala, which is a critical brain area involved in processing and expressing human emotions and fear reactions. Such transformations may lead to greater emotional reactivity and managing the negative emotions, which might be among the factors contributing to the symptoms known to be presented by trauma survivors, for instance, hypervigilance and emotional dysregulation.

Moreover, trauma often involves the ability to impact the prefrontal cortex, a region that performs executive functions, including decision-making, impulse control, and flexibility. Recent neuroimaging studies demonstrated that trauma-induced alterations in the prefrontal cortex may distort the ability of an individual to be able to control their emotions and behavior when they are exposed to stressors that consequently cause failure to use adaptive responses. The disconnection between the prefrontal cortex and other brain areas, including the amygdala and hippocampus that impair emotional processing can be another area that further contributes to the challenge of emotion regulation.

Learning the role of neuroplasticity in trauma may open the gate to the mechanisms involving the development or withholding of trauma-related psychopathology. The brain being able to change thanks to trauma is both a maladaptive change and also presents humans with opportunities to heal and recover. Interventions like trauma-focused therapy and mindfulness-based practices have been ascertained to be beneficial in terms of promoting key needed neuroplastic changes in the brain that foster resilience and stimulate adaptive coping strategies. Through the power of neuroplasticity, trauma survivors are able to create new narratives that let them focus on what they can do to manage their emotions rather than the events that happened to them. They also develop a deeper sense of self and start to move forward with their lives empowered and in control. So, showing the role of neuroplasticity emphasizes that trauma-informed approaches must be developed because the brain is predestined to change and adapt, which is going to support continued recovery and well-being.

The Concept of Somatic Experiencing

Somatic experiencing is a therapy that addresses a body's ability to heal from trauma by feeling and dealing with sensations that arise through the lived body. Grounded in the realization that trauma is not only psychological but also physiological, somatic experiencing is based on the importance of focusing one's attention on the physical entrance of trauma into a person's body. Implementing somatic experiencing makes it possible for individuals to become attuned to the internal body responses, which may include muscle tightness, pain, and discomfort, for instance, and to create mind-body connections by understanding how these body responses can relate to past traumatic experiences. Expressing these feelings and mastering their control is the gradual way of freeing the energy that is deeply tied to the trauma and consequently healing the split.

Central to Somatic Experiencing is the concept of titration, which means a little bit more exploring the traumatic memories and bodily sensations gradually, without over-excitement of the nervous system. Instead of going into the depth of tragedy, somatic experience practitioners lead their clients through small steps of minuscule sizes that gradually build resilience and tolerance over time to distressing experiences. It, therefore, contributes to avoiding further traumatization, and it makes quiet and slow work possible so that the nervous system can process and integrate the traumatic memories and sensations in a safe environment. By means of titration, the patients will be able to carefully build up the span of pain and sorrow that they can tolerate, allowing them to heal themselves in an understanding and compassionate way.

Additionally, the somatic experiencing theory gives significance to resuming the response of the body to trauma that may have been stopped or blocked due to the initial traumatic event. Through the gradual guidance of persons to reassert and release the survival energies that have taken origin during traumatic events, somatic experiencing shall enable the nervous system to reevaluate, reset, and eventually return to a state of balance. With the help of pendulation and resourcing, people are trained to exercise and enhance their inborn capabilities that support self-regulation and indomitability. The outcome of such practice enables the sustainability of a sound mind and healthy body. In this case, Somatic Experiencing offers a groundbreaking model by focusing on and viewing the body as the vessel of wisdom and the route toward recovery and wholeness.

Mental And Physical Aspects Of Trauma For Comprehensive Healing

Recognizing and addressing both the mental and physical aspects of trauma is paramount for achieving comprehensive healing and restoring overall well-being. Trauma affects individuals on multiple levels, encompassing psychological, physiological, and even spiritual dimensions. Neglecting either the mental or physical aspects of trauma can hinder the healing process and perpetuate lingering symptoms and distress. By acknowledging the interconnectedness of these aspects, individuals and healthcare professionals can adopt a holistic approach that addresses the full spectrum of trauma's impact, leading to more effective and sustainable outcomes.

On the mental front, trauma can manifest in various ways, including intrusive thoughts, flashbacks, anxiety, depression, and difficulties in regulating emotions. These psychological symptoms often stem from underlying disruptions in cognitive processing, emotional regulation, and interpersonal functioning. Addressing the mental aspects of trauma involves providing individuals with tools and strategies to navigate their thoughts and emotions, challenge maladaptive beliefs, and cultivate resilience. Therapeutic interventions such as cognitive-behavioral therapy (CBT), eye movement desensitization and reprocessing (EMDR), and dialectical behavior therapy (DBT) can help individuals process traumatic memories, develop coping skills, and rebuild a sense of safety and empowerment.

Simultaneously, it's crucial to recognize and address the physical manifestations of trauma, which can include chronic pain, somatic symptoms, and disruptions in autonomic nervous system functioning. Trauma can dysregulate various physiological systems, leading to heightened arousal, inflammation, and alterations in hormonal balance. Neglecting the physical aspects of trauma can perpetuate physical discomfort and exacerbate psychological distress, as the body and mind are intricately interconnected. Integrative approaches such as somatic experiencing, yoga, acupuncture, and massage therapy offer valuable avenues for addressing the physiological effects of trauma and promoting relaxation, restoration, and physical well-being. By attending to both the mental and physical dimensions of trauma, individuals can embark on a comprehensive healing journey that fosters integration, resilience, and a renewed sense of wholeness.

The Importance of a Holistic Approach

The Limitations of Traditional Approaches

Traditional approaches to trauma treatment often prioritize addressing the psychological aspects of trauma while overlooking the interconnected physical and physiological dimensions. By solely focusing on psychological symptoms such as intrusive thoughts, nightmares, and avoidance behaviors, these approaches may neglect the profound impact of trauma on the body and the nervous system. Consequently, trauma survivors may continue to experience physical symptoms such as chronic pain, gastrointestinal disturbances, and sleep disturbances, which can exacerbate psychological distress and hinder the healing process. Moreover, traditional approaches may fail to consider the role of social and environmental factors in shaping individuals' experiences of trauma, overlooking the importance of addressing systemic inequalities and promoting social support networks in trauma recovery.

Furthermore, traditional approaches to trauma treatment often rely heavily on talk therapy and cognitive-based interventions, which may not be suitable for all individuals, particularly those with limited verbal communication skills or cultural backgrounds that prioritize somatic expression. This one-size-fits-all approach may inadvertently marginalize certain populations and perpetuate disparities in access to effective trauma care. Additionally, traditional approaches may overlook the role of implicit memory and the body's role in storing traumatic experiences, leading to incomplete processing and integration of traumatic memories. Without addressing the somatic and physiological aspects of trauma, individuals may struggle to fully heal and may continue to experience symptoms of distress and dysregulation.

Moreover, traditional approaches may inadvertently reinforce the stigma surrounding mental health issues and discourage individuals from seeking help due to fears of being labeled as "mentally ill." This stigma can further isolate trauma survivors and prevent them from accessing the support and resources they need to heal. Additionally, traditional approaches may overlook the importance of empowerment and self-advocacy in trauma recovery, instead fostering a dependency on external sources of validation and support. By recognizing the limitations of traditional approaches and embracing a more holistic and inclusive framework that addresses the multidimensional nature of trauma, healthcare professionals can better support trauma survivors in their journey toward healing and resilience.

Advocate For an Integrative Approach

Advocating for an integrative approach to trauma treatment entails recognizing the inherent interconnectedness of physical, emotional, and spiritual well-being in the healing process. Trauma affects individuals on multiple levels, permeating their thoughts, emotions, behaviors, and bodily sensations. Therefore, addressing trauma requires a comprehensive understanding of the whole person and the unique ways in which they experience and respond to traumatic experiences. An integrative approach acknowledges that trauma recovery involves more than just alleviating symptoms; it entails promoting holistic well-being and empowering individuals to reclaim agency over their lives.

Incorporating physical, emotional, and spiritual dimensions into trauma treatment allows for a more personalized and holistic approach that meets individuals' diverse needs and preferences. While traditional therapeutic modalities may focus primarily on addressing psychological symptoms, an integrative approach recognizes the importance of attending to physical sensations, such as tension, pain, and discomfort, which are often manifestations of trauma stored in the body. By integrating somatic-based interventions such as yoga, mindfulness, and bodywork into trauma treatment, individuals can learn to regulate their nervous systems, release trapped energy, and cultivate a deeper connection with their bodies, fostering a sense of groundedness and resilience.

Furthermore, an integrative approach acknowledges the spiritual dimension of trauma recovery, recognizing that trauma can profoundly impact individuals' sense of meaning, purpose, and connection to self and others. By incorporating practices that nurture individuals' spiritual well-being, such as meditation, contemplative prayer, and expressive arts therapy, trauma treatment can foster a sense of inner peace, acceptance, and transcendence. Embracing spirituality in trauma recovery offers individuals a framework for making sense of their experiences, finding meaning in their suffering, and accessing inner resources for healing and transformation. Ultimately, advocating for an integrative approach that considers the whole person empowers trauma survivors to embark on a journey toward comprehensive healing, restoration, and empowerment.

The Effectiveness of Complementary Therapies

Complementary therapies, including yoga, meditation, acupuncture, and massage, have emerged as powerful adjunctive tools in trauma recovery, offering unique pathways for healing and resilience. These modalities operate on the principle of addressing the interconnectedness of mind, body, and spirit, facilitating holistic well-being and promoting self-regulation. Yoga, for instance, combines physical postures, breathwork, and mindfulness practices to cultivate awareness of bodily sensations and promote relaxation and grounding. By incorporating gentle movement and breathing exercises, individuals can release tension stored in the body, regulate their nervous systems, and foster a sense of embodiment and empowerment.

Similarly, meditation offers individuals a means of cultivating present-moment awareness and fostering self-compassion and acceptance. Mindfulness practices encourage individuals to observe their thoughts and emotions without judgment, allowing them to develop greater resilience and emotional regulation skills. By incorporating meditation into trauma recovery, individuals can learn to cultivate a sense of inner calm and balance, even amidst distressing experiences. Acupuncture, an ancient healing modality rooted in traditional Chinese medicine, involves the insertion of thin needles into specific points on the body to stimulate energy flow and restore balance. Acupuncture has been shown to reduce symptoms of anxiety, depression, and post-traumatic stress disorder (PTSD), offering individuals a non-invasive and holistic approach to managing trauma-related symptoms.

Furthermore, massage therapy offers individuals a safe and nurturing space to release tension, promote relaxation, and restore a sense of connection with their bodies. Through gentle touch and manipulation of soft tissues, massage therapy can alleviate physical discomfort, soothe the nervous system, and enhance feelings of safety and trust. By integrating complementary therapies such as yoga, meditation, acupuncture, and massage into trauma recovery, individuals can access additional tools and resources for healing and empowerment. These modalities offer individuals a holistic approach to trauma recovery that addresses the interconnected physical, emotional, and spiritual dimensions of their experiences, fostering resilience, restoration, and renewed hope for the future.

Kenny Ajayi

The Importance Of Addressing Social Determinants Of Health In Trauma Treatment

Addressing social determinants of health, such as socioeconomic status and access to resources, is paramount in trauma treatment to ensure equitable access to care and promote comprehensive healing. Trauma disproportionately affects marginalized communities who may face systemic barriers to accessing quality healthcare, mental health services, and social support networks. Individuals from low-income backgrounds or minority groups may experience heightened levels of stress, discrimination, and adversity, exacerbating the impact of trauma on their mental and physical well-being. By recognizing and addressing these social determinants of health, trauma treatment can be tailored to meet the unique needs and challenges faced by individuals from diverse backgrounds, ultimately promoting more equitable outcomes and fostering inclusive healing environments.

Moreover, socioeconomic status and access to resources profoundly influence individuals' ability to access trauma-informed care and engage in self-care practices. Limited financial resources may hinder individuals' access to mental health services, medications, and other essential resources needed for recovery. Additionally, individuals living in underserved communities may face geographical barriers to accessing trauma treatment, such as limited transportation options or a shortage of healthcare providers. By addressing structural inequalities and advocating for policies that promote equitable access to healthcare and social services, trauma treatment can mitigate disparities in outcomes and improve the overall well-being of marginalized populations.

Furthermore, social support networks and community resources play a crucial role in facilitating trauma recovery and promoting resilience. Individuals with strong social support systems may have access to tangible and emotional support from friends, family members, and community organizations, which can buffer the effects of trauma and foster a sense of belonging and connectedness. Conversely, individuals lacking social support may experience increased feelings of isolation, loneliness, and helplessness, which can exacerbate trauma-related symptoms and hinder recovery. By fostering inclusive and supportive communities that prioritize empathy, compassion, and mutual aid, trauma treatment can empower individuals to heal and thrive despite adversity, emphasizing the importance of addressing social determinants of health in promoting holistic well-being and resilience.

Encourage Collaboration Among Healthcare Professionals

Encouraging collaboration among healthcare professionals from diverse disciplines is essential to providing comprehensive care for trauma survivors. Trauma affects individuals on multiple levels, encompassing physical, psychological, social, and spiritual dimensions. No single discipline possesses all the expertise necessary to address the complex needs of trauma survivors adequately. Therefore, interdisciplinary collaboration allows healthcare professionals to pool their knowledge, skills, and resources to provide holistic and personalized care tailored to each individual's unique needs and experiences. By bringing together professionals from fields such as psychology, psychiatry, social work, nursing, and complementary medicine, trauma survivors can benefit from a comprehensive and coordinated approach to healing and recovery.

Furthermore, interdisciplinary collaboration fosters a more holistic understanding of trauma and its effects on individuals' lives. Each discipline brings its own perspectives, frameworks, and interventions to the table, enriching the overall understanding of trauma and promoting innovative approaches to treatment. For example, psychologists may provide evidence-based therapies such as cognitive-behavioral therapy (CBT) or eye movement desensitization and reprocessing (EMDR) to address psychological symptoms, while social workers may connect individuals with community resources and support networks to address social determinants of health. By integrating these diverse perspectives and approaches, healthcare professionals can develop more comprehensive treatment plans that address the multifaceted nature of trauma and promote long-term healing and resilience.

Moreover, interdisciplinary collaboration promotes continuity of care and reduces fragmentation in the healthcare system, ensuring that trauma survivors receive seamless and coordinated support across different stages of their recovery journey. By working collaboratively, healthcare professionals can share information, coordinate referrals, and provide ongoing support to individuals as they navigate the complexities of trauma recovery. Additionally, interdisciplinary teams can facilitate communication and collaboration between different healthcare settings, such as hospitals, clinics, and community-based organizations, ensuring that trauma survivors have access to a continuum of care that addresses their evolving needs over time. Overall, encouraging collaboration among healthcare professionals from diverse disciplines is essential to providing trauma survivors with the comprehensive care and support they need to heal and thrive.

Final Thoughts and The Way Forward

The Resilience and Strength of Trauma Survivors

Acknowledging the resilience and strength of trauma survivors is essential in recognizing their courage and perseverance in the face of adversity. Trauma can shatter individuals' sense of safety, trust, and stability, leaving lasting emotional scars and challenging their ability to cope with daily life. Despite these immense challenges, trauma survivors demonstrate remarkable resilience and adaptability as they navigate their healing journeys. They draw upon their inner resources, resilience, and support networks to confront their trauma, rebuild their lives, and find meaning and purpose amidst their pain. By acknowledging and honoring the resilience of trauma survivors, we validate their experiences, instill hope, and empower them to embrace their strengths and resilience as they continue on their path toward healing and wholeness.

Moreover, recognizing the resilience of trauma survivors serves as a powerful counter-narrative to the pervasive stigma and stereotypes surrounding trauma and mental health issues. Too often, individuals who have experienced trauma are unfairly labeled as "victims" or "broken," perpetuating misconceptions about their capabilities and potential for recovery. By highlighting the resilience and strength of trauma survivors, we challenge these harmful stereotypes and promote a more compassionate and empathetic understanding of trauma. Trauma survivors are not defined by their experiences; they are individuals with agency, resilience, and the capacity to heal and thrive despite their past traumas. By acknowledging and celebrating their resilience, we affirm their dignity, worth, and inherent capacity for growth and transformation.

Furthermore, acknowledging the resilience of trauma survivors fosters a culture of support, validation, and empowerment within communities and healthcare systems. When trauma survivors feel seen, heard, and valued, they are more likely to seek help, engage in treatment, and advocate for their needs. By creating safe and supportive environments that honor and celebrate the resilience of trauma survivors, we foster a sense of belonging and connection that is essential for healing and recovery. Moreover, by amplifying the voices and stories of trauma survivors, we inspire others to recognize their own resilience and seek support when needed. Ultimately, acknowledging the resilience of trauma survivors is not only a gesture of compassion and solidarity but also a catalyst for positive change and healing within ourselves and our communities.

Destigmatizing Mental Health Issues And Promoting Open Dialogue

Advocating for the destigmatization of mental health issues and fostering open dialogue about trauma experiences is crucial in creating supportive and inclusive communities where individuals feel safe to seek help and share their stories without fear of judgment or discrimination. The stigma surrounding mental health issues often prevents individuals from seeking the support and resources they need to address trauma-related symptoms and heal from their experiences. This stigma can manifest in various forms, including societal attitudes, cultural beliefs, and institutional barriers, all of which contribute to the marginalization and exclusion of trauma survivors. By challenging these stigmatizing attitudes and promoting open dialogue about mental health and trauma, we can create a more compassionate and understanding society that values and supports the well-being of all its members.

Furthermore, destigmatizing mental health issues and encouraging open dialogue about trauma experiences can help reduce feelings of shame, isolation, and self-blame often experienced by trauma survivors. When individuals feel empowered to speak openly about their struggles and seek support from others, they are more likely to access timely and effective treatment, leading to better outcomes and improved quality of life. By creating spaces for individuals to share their stories, express their emotions, and connect with others who have had similar experiences, we foster a sense of community and solidarity that is essential for healing and resilience. Moreover, promoting open dialogue about trauma can help raise awareness, increase understanding, and challenge misconceptions about mental health issues, ultimately paving the way for more compassionate and inclusive attitudes toward trauma survivors.

Additionally, advocating for destigmatization and open dialogue about trauma experiences is a critical step toward promoting systemic change and improving access to trauma-informed care and support services. The stigma surrounding mental health issues often leads to underfunding, inadequate resources, and disparities in access to care within healthcare systems and communities. By advocating for policies and initiatives that prioritize mental health and trauma awareness, we can create more equitable and inclusive systems that address the needs of all individuals, regardless of their background or circumstances. Moreover, by amplifying the voices and stories of trauma survivors, we can inspire others to join the movement for change and create a future where mental health is recognized as a fundamental human right and where all individuals have the support and resources they need to heal and thrive.

The Importance of Ongoing Support Networks and Community Resources

Stressing the importance of ongoing support networks and community resources for trauma survivors is essential in fostering healing, resilience, and long-term recovery. Trauma can profoundly impact individuals' sense of safety, trust, and connection with others, leading to feelings of isolation, loneliness, and alienation. Ongoing support networks provide trauma survivors with a sense of belonging and validation, allowing them to share their experiences, express their emotions, and receive support from others who have had similar experiences. These networks can include friends, family members, support groups, online communities, and peer support programs, all of which offer opportunities for individuals to connect, empathize, and learn from one another, ultimately reducing feelings of isolation and promoting a sense of solidarity and empowerment.

Furthermore, community resources play a crucial role in providing trauma survivors with access to essential services and support that address their diverse needs and circumstances. Community-based organizations, mental health clinics, advocacy groups, and crisis hotlines offer trauma survivors a wide range of resources, including counseling, therapy, crisis intervention, legal advocacy, housing assistance, and financial support. By collaborating with community partners and stakeholders, healthcare professionals can help connect trauma survivors with the resources and services they need to address their trauma-related symptoms, rebuild their lives, and navigate the challenges of daily living. Additionally, community resources can play a vital role in promoting prevention and early intervention efforts, raising awareness about trauma and its effects, and advocating for policies and initiatives that support trauma survivors and promote social justice and equity.

Moreover, ongoing support networks and community resources provide trauma survivors with opportunities for empowerment, agency, and advocacy. By participating in support groups, peer mentoring programs, and community organizing efforts, trauma survivors can become agents of change and leaders in their own healing journeys. These experiences allow individuals to develop resilience, build self-esteem, and reclaim a sense of control over their lives, ultimately empowering them to advocate for their rights, access resources, and create positive change within their communities. By stressing the importance of ongoing support networks and community resources, we can foster a culture of empathy, compassion, and solidarity that supports trauma survivors in their journey toward healing, resilience, and empowerment.

The Need for Continued Research
And Innovation in Trauma Treatment

The need for continued research and innovation in trauma treatment is paramount to address the evolving nature of trauma and its complex effects on individuals' lives. Trauma is a multifaceted phenomenon with diverse manifestations, impacting individuals' physical, emotional, social, and spiritual well-being. Therefore, ongoing research is essential to deepen our understanding of the underlying mechanisms of trauma, identify risk factors and protective factors, and develop effective interventions that address the diverse needs and experiences of trauma survivors. By investing in research, we can advance our knowledge of trauma and its effects, leading to more targeted and personalized treatment approaches that improve outcomes and accessibility for all individuals affected by trauma.

Moreover, continued research and innovation in trauma treatment are essential to address existing gaps and disparities in access to care and support services. Despite growing awareness of trauma and its impact, many individuals still face barriers to accessing timely and culturally competent care. These barriers can include limited availability of trauma-informed services, lack of trained professionals, financial constraints, and stigma surrounding mental health issues. By conducting research on strategies to improve access to trauma treatment, such as telehealth, peer support programs, and community-based interventions, we can identify effective solutions that increase accessibility and reduce disparities in care. Additionally, research can inform policy development and advocacy efforts aimed at expanding funding, resources, and support for trauma survivors and promoting systemic change within healthcare systems and communities.

Furthermore, continued research and innovation in trauma treatment are essential to address emerging challenges and trends in trauma care. As our understanding of trauma evolves, so too must our treatment approaches to meet the evolving needs of trauma survivors. For example, research on the impact of trauma on specific populations, such as veterans, children, refugees, and LGBTQ+ individuals, can inform the development of culturally sensitive and age-appropriate interventions that address their unique experiences and needs. Additionally, research on the integration of complementary therapies, technology-based interventions, and novel treatment modalities, such as virtual reality therapy and psychedelic-assisted therapy, holds promise for enhancing the effectiveness and accessibility of trauma treatment. By fostering a culture of innovation and collaboration, we can continue to push the boundaries of what is possible in trauma treatment and ensure that all individuals affected by trauma have access to the care and support they need to heal and thrive.

Practical Suggestions for Self-Care Practices and Coping Strategies

Self-care practices and coping strategies play a vital role in promoting resilience and well-being for both trauma survivors and their supporters. For trauma survivors, it's crucial to prioritize self-care activities that foster a sense of safety, stability, and empowerment. This may include establishing a routine that incorporates healthy habits such as regular exercise, nutritious eating, and adequate sleep. Engaging in activities that promote relaxation and stress reduction, such as mindfulness meditation, deep breathing exercises, and progressive muscle relaxation, can help individuals regulate their emotions and alleviate symptoms of anxiety and hypervigilance. Additionally, creative outlets such as journaling, art therapy, and music can provide a means of self-expression and processing traumatic experiences in a safe and supportive environment.

For supporters of trauma survivors, it's essential to practice self-care to prevent burnout and compassion fatigue. Providing support to trauma survivors can be emotionally demanding and draining, making it crucial for supporters to prioritize their own well-being and replenish their energy reserves. This may involve setting boundaries and limits on caregiving responsibilities, seeking support from friends, family members, or support groups, and engaging in activities that bring joy and fulfillment outside of their caregiving role. Practicing self-compassion and self-acceptance and recognizing that it's okay to ask for help and take breaks when needed can help supporters maintain their resilience and effectiveness in supporting trauma survivors over the long term.

Moreover, fostering a sense of community and connection is essential for both trauma survivors and their supporters. Building and maintaining supportive relationships with others who understand and validate their experiences can provide a sense of belonging and reduce feelings of isolation and loneliness. This may involve participating in support groups, attending therapy sessions, or joining online communities where individuals can share their stories, offer support, and receive encouragement from others who have had similar experiences. By nurturing these connections and building a network of support, trauma survivors and their supporters can find strength, inspiration, and validation in each other's journeys, ultimately promoting healing, resilience, and empowerment for all involved.

Hope for The Future

Highlighting stories of resilience and recovery can inspire hope for the future by demonstrating that healing is possible even in the face of adversity. These stories serve as powerful reminders of the human capacity to overcome challenges, grow from experiences, and rebuild lives after trauma. By sharing narratives of individuals who have navigated their healing journeys with courage, perseverance, and resilience, we instill hope in others who may be struggling with their own trauma-related issues. These stories illustrate that recovery is not a linear process and that setbacks and struggles are a natural part of the journey. However, they also showcase the transformative power of resilience, inner strength, and support in overcoming obstacles and reclaiming agency over one's life.

Moreover, stories of resilience and recovery highlight the importance of support networks, community resources, and compassionate care in promoting healing and well-being. These narratives often feature individuals who have benefited from the support of friends, family members, mental health professionals, and community organizations in their recovery journey. By showcasing the positive impact of these supportive relationships and resources, we underscore the importance of fostering a culture of empathy, understanding, and solidarity that validates and uplifts trauma survivors. These stories also serve as a call to action for communities and healthcare systems to prioritize trauma-informed care, destigmatize mental health issues, and promote access to resources and support services for all individuals affected by trauma.

Furthermore, stories of resilience and recovery offer hope for the future by challenging stigma, raising awareness, and promoting societal change. By amplifying the voices and experiences of trauma survivors, we challenge misconceptions and stereotypes surrounding trauma and mental health issues, fostering a more compassionate and inclusive society. These stories inspire individuals to speak out, seek help, and advocate for their rights, ultimately paving the way for systemic change within healthcare systems, communities, and society at large. By sharing stories of resilience and recovery, we create a ripple effect of hope, healing, and empowerment that extends far beyond individual narratives, transforming attitudes, policies, and practices to better support the well-being and dignity of all individuals affected by trauma.

Advocacy Efforts to Promote Policies

Encouraging advocacy efforts to promote policies that support trauma-informed care and prevention initiatives is crucial in creating systemic change and fostering a culture of empathy, understanding, and support for trauma survivors. Trauma-informed care recognizes the pervasive impact of trauma on individuals' lives and seeks to create environments that are sensitive to the needs and experiences of trauma survivors. By advocating for policies that prioritize trauma-informed practices within healthcare systems, educational institutions, social services, and other settings, we can ensure that trauma survivors receive the compassionate and comprehensive care and support they deserve. This may involve advocating for training and education for healthcare professionals and service providers on trauma awareness, trauma-informed approaches, and evidence-based treatment modalities. Additionally, advocating for policies that promote trauma-informed practices in schools, workplaces, and community organizations can create safer and more supportive environments for individuals affected by trauma, ultimately reducing the risk of retraumatization and promoting healing and resilience.

Furthermore, advocating for prevention initiatives is essential in addressing the root causes of trauma and reducing its incidence in the first place. Prevention efforts may include promoting early intervention programs, mental health screenings, and educational campaigns aimed at raising awareness about trauma and its effects. By advocating for policies that address social determinants of health, such as poverty, discrimination, and violence, we can create more equitable and inclusive societies where individuals are less vulnerable to trauma. Additionally, advocating for policies that address systemic inequalities and promote social justice can help address the underlying structural factors that contribute to trauma, such as racism, sexism, and economic inequality. By advocating for prevention initiatives that address these root causes, we can create healthier and more resilient communities where individuals have the support and resources they need to thrive.

Moreover, encouraging advocacy efforts to promote policies that support trauma-informed care and prevention initiatives can help amplify the voices and experiences of trauma survivors, empowering them to become agents of change in their own healing journeys. By partnering with grassroots organizations, advocacy groups, and community leaders, trauma survivors can advocate for policies that reflect their needs and priorities, ensuring that their voices are heard and their rights are protected. Additionally, by mobilizing public support and building coalitions with like-minded allies, advocates can create momentum for policy change and hold decision-makers accountable for prioritizing trauma-informed care and prevention efforts. Ultimately, encouraging advocacy efforts to promote policies that support trauma-informed care and prevention initiatives is a powerful way to create systemic change and build a more compassionate, resilient, and supportive society for all individuals affected by trauma.

About the Author

Kenny Ajayi was born in October 1994 in Chicago, IL, and is the oldest of four siblings. In high school, he took part in extracurricular activities, including drama club, and played sports such as baseball. He was accepted into the National Honor Society (NHS), graduated high school with a 3.33, and was ranked in the top 10% of his class. He was bullied in school and has experienced depression, self-harm, eating disorders, and body dysmorphia. He went to college to study Theatre and got his degree in that field. His hobbies are acting, painting, and reading and writing short stories in his spare time. His interests are modeling and becoming an activist for anti-bullying/mental health. He loves to workout, participate in volunteer work and nature, like recycling to save the planet.

The reason for this book: I wrote this book for anyone out there struggling with any kind of mental health or trauma, whether it's anxiety, depression, being abused, being bullied anywhere, etc. I want people to know that they're not alone and they can go to a clinic for any type of treatment. This book is targeted at people related to these types of issues (young adults in particular). Hopefully, this book inspires them.